KU-310-242

# 1980s Unemployment and the Unions

*Essays on the impotent price structure of Britain and monopoly in the labour market*

## F. A. HAYEK, CH
*Nobel Laureate 1974*

With a Postscript on British Trade Unions and the Law:

### From Taff Vale to Tebbit

by

## CHARLES G. HANSON
*Lecturer in Economics,*
*University of Newcastle upon Tyne*

*Published by*

THE INSTITUTE OF ECONOMIC AFFAIRS

1980

SECOND EDITION 1984

*First published in December 1980*
*Second Edition July 1984*
*by*
The Institute of Economic Affairs
2 Lord North Street, Westminster,
London SW1P 3LB

© THE INSTITUTE OF ECONOMIC AFFAIRS 1980 and 1984

*All rights reserved*

ISSN 0073-2818
ISBN 0-255 36173-4

*Printed in England by*
GORON PRO-PRINT CO LTD
*6 Marlborough Road, Churchill Industrial Estate, Lancing, Sussex*

*Text set in 'Monotype' Baskerville*

# CONTENTS

PART IV.

## The Trade Unions and Britain's Economic Decline

# PREFACE

The *Hobart Papers* are intended to contribute a stream of authoritative, independent and lucid analyses to the understanding and application of economics to private and government activity. The characteristic theme has been the optimum use of scarce resources and the extent to which it can best be achieved in markets within an appropriate framework or, where markets cannot work, in other ways. Since the alternative to the market is, in practice, the state, and both are imperfect, the choice between them should effectively depend on judgement of the comparative consequences of 'market failure' and 'government failure'.

Hobart Paper 87 is an analysis by the Austrian-born but since 1938 British economist, F. A. Hayek, of the most stubborn obstacle to the efficient working of markets in the British economy: the main cause of the decline of the economic system.

The *Paper* includes three considerably re-written Parts, II, III and IV, based on material used in BBC broadcasts in 1978. The text has been expanded to explain the argument more fully than was possible in the 'air-time' then available, and examples have been added to illustrate the argument.

Part I reviews the essence of the argument elaborated in the succeeding essays.

Part II is an analysis of the elementary but fundamental principles governing the distribution of scarce resources to meet consumer demands. It demonstrates the rôle of the market as a device for signalling changes in supply and demand and the required redistribution of resources. Here Professor Hayek emphasises that people use their resources to produce commodities or services for people unknown to them; that there is no adequate substitute for the signalling rôle of prices in guiding producers to the wants, preferences or demands of their unknown consumers. The reasoning here is simple and clear enough for the non-economist but contains penetrating insights into the working of economic systems that are designed to serve the consumer, whether under capitalism or under

[7]

socialism or communism. He points, for example, to the statistical nonsense of measuring production by the costs of its input of labour and capital rather than by the value of its output, to the political nonsense of job creation that instead creates unemployment, and to the economic nonsense, taught by Keynes and his followers, of supposing that employment can be maintained at full stretch by bolstering total demand. He points to the implication that the real cause of the 'de-industrialisation' now loudly lamented by British politicians is essentially the inflation of costs that has made the products of British industry unsaleable.

Part III examines three alternative policies on the attitudes to, and the use of, markets. The first is to refine the framework of law, especially to corral social costs known by the economists' jargon of 'externalities'. The second is to attempt to direct economic activity from the centre. This method is ineffective unless there is agreement on the objectives of policy, which is possible only by coercion in a socialised society, but not in a free society with a maximum of individual liberty. The third alternative is to remove the domination of the market by monopoly—whether in the corporativism of employers and employees in collusion with government or in the syndicalism of trade unions.

In this discussion Professor Hayek covers the futility of 'incomes policies'; the power of the market to minimise coercion; the difficulty of reconciling the most effective reward for effort with a 'just' reward; the superiority of a system guided by abstract rules in serving the consumer over a system in which there is deliberate pursuit of the interests of known people; the contrast between primitive society with more scope for altruism and industrial society with more scope for removing poverty; the conflict between high-mindedness and the maximisation of wealth to raise living standards; the error of Keynes, dramatised by the poet who wrote that aiming for heaven makes life hell. And Professor Hayek shows the relevance of these insights for Britain.

Part IV then applies the economic analysis of the necessity for market signalling to the labour market in Britain. Examination of the powers given to the trade unions by the privileges conferred by trade union law, and their effects on wage differentials, unemployment, inflation and general economic decline, lead Professor Hayek to the conclusion that the British labour

[8]

market, and the British market economy as a whole, no longer tells the people of Britain where to use their resources because it has severely blunted the rewards for using them correctly and the penalties for using them wrongly.

Part V is a slightly edited version of an article in *The Times* of 10 October 1978 which describes the conditions of the British economy as Professor Hayek then saw it. His judgement in November 1980 is indicated in Part I.

This *Hobart Paper* sums up the teaching of a lifetime on the rôle of trade unions in a free society that Professor Hayek has patiently refined down the years, during many of which he was ignored or condemned, until the recent past when his thinking has begun to be seen as inconvenient but inescapable. The Institute's constitution requires it to dissociate its Trustees, Directors and Advisers from the analyses of its authors. In 1980 Professor Hayek's work stands unique.

*November 1980*                                         ARTHUR SELDON

## PREFACE TO THE SECOND EDITION, 1984

In the $3\frac{1}{2}$ years since the First Edition of Hobart Paper 87, Parliament has taken the early steps to remove the legal power that enables British trade unions to damage the economy, often to the disadvantage of their members (and their families) as well as non-unionised employees. In a Postscript to this Second Edition, Dr Charles Hanson—who has made himself an authority on British trade union law—assesses those steps and argues for more.

The outdated notion that the trade unions are spokesmen for the underdog has inhibited British governments from removing the nearly 80-year-old legal privileges that have strengthened unions' power to act as vested interests defending outdated occupations and restrictive practices in declining industries. Dr Hanson indicates that the reforms so far are the beginning, and the end is not yet in sight. He specifically argues that more requires to be done urgently to remove immunities and introduce no-strike contracts in essential 'public' (a euphemism for state or government) or private monopoly employment. Moreover, as the 1984 miners' strike has dramatised, the law on secondary picketing, which in practice has not been generally applied, requires further reform to include secondary strikes at the places of work of suppliers or customers of firms in dispute. These reforms, Dr Hanson argues, will go far to meet Professor Hayek's critique of trade union legal privileges.

Dr Hanson argues that privileges should also be removed from the professions. A further measure that is indispensable to complement legal reform is that of removing the power of 'public' (state, government) employers to absorb increases in labour costs not earned by higher output. The power of labour combinations, among manual or professional workers, rests not only on legal power but ultimately on market power. Legal reform leaves untouched the power of trade unions or professional associations, of coal miners or doctors, railwaymen or teachers, to enforce their demands on monopoly 'public' employers in fuel and transport, education and medicine, in contrast to their opposite numbers in competitive private industry. Legal reform may therefore benefit the consumer of private goods and services but leave the taxpayer, who finances 'public' (state, government) goods and services, to continue to suffer under the collusive acts of monopoly 'public' employers and their employees' associations. Legal reform is not enough: it must be buttressed by dissolving the artificial coagulation of 'public' market power by subjecting it to competition in the market.

This Second Edition is Professor Hayek's first publication in Britain since the Queen's Birthday Award of the dignity of Companion of Honour (CH) for his 'services to the study of economics'. This is the first public British honour since the Swedish award of the Nobel Prize 10 years ago, in 1974. It is a fitting recognition, at the age of 85, of the economist (and much else), British by choice rather than accident of birth, who has emerged as the world's leading exponent of classical English and Scottish political economy.

*June 1984*                                    ARTHUR SELDON

# FRONTISPIECE

'It may perhaps be pointed out that it has, of course, never been denied that employment can be rapidly increased, and a position of "full employment" achieved in the shortest possible time, by means of monetary expansion—least of all by those economists whose outlook has been influenced by the experience of a major inflation. All that has been contended is that the kind of full employment which can be created in this way is inherently unstable, and that to create employment by these means is to perpetuate fluctuations. There may be desperate situations in which it may indeed be necessary to increase employment at all costs, even if it be only for a short period—perhaps the situation in which Dr Brüning found himself in Germany in 1932 was such a situation in which desperate means would have been justified. But the economist should not conceal the fact that to aim at the maximum of employment which can be achieved in the short run by means of monetary policy is essentially the policy of the desperado who has nothing to lose and everything to gain from a short breathing space.'
[F. A. HAYEK, *Profits, Interest and Investment* (1939), p. 630.]

'The truth is that by a mistaken theoretical view we have been led into a precarious position in which we cannot prevent substantial unemployment from re-appearing: not because, as my view is sometimes misrepresented, this unemployment is deliberately brought about as a means to combat inflation, but because it is now bound to appear as a deeply regrettable but *inescapable* consequence of the mistaken policies of the past as soon as inflation ceases to accelerate.' [F. A. HAYEK, 'The Pretence of Knowledge', Nobel Memorial Prize Lecture 1974, reprinted in *Full Employment at Any Price?*, Occasional Paper 45, IEA, 1975, quotation from p. 37.]

## THE AUTHOR

Friedrich August Hayek, Dr Jur, Dr Sc Pol (Vienna), DSc (Econ.) (London), Visiting Professor at the University of Salzburg, Austria, 1970-74. Director of the Austrian Institute for Economic Research, 1927-31, and Lecturer in Economics at the University of Vienna, 1929-31. Tooke Professor of Economic Science and Statistics, University of London, 1931-50. Professor of Social and Moral Science, University of Chicago, 1950-62. Professor of Economics, University of Freiburg i.Brg., West Germany, 1962-68. He was awarded the Alfred Nobel Memorial Prize in Economic Science in 1974. He was appointed Companion of Honour in the Queen's Birthday Honours in June 1984.

Professor Hayek's most important publications include *Prices and Production* (1931), *Monetary Theory and the Trade Cycle* (1933), *The Pure Theory of Capital* (1941), *The Road to Serfdom* (1944), *Individualism and Economic Order* (1948), *The Counter-Revolution of Science* (1952), and *The Constitution of Liberty* (1960). His latest works are collections of his writings under the titles *Studies in Philosophy, Politics and Economics* (1967), *New Studies in Philosophy, Politics, Economics and the History of Ideas* (1978), and *Law, Legislation and Liberty* (Vol. I: *Rules and Order*, 1973; Vol. II: *The Mirage of Social Justice*, 1976; Vol. III: *The Political Order of a Free People*, 1979). He has also edited several books and has published articles in the *Economic Journal*, *Economica* and other journals.

The IEA has published his *The Confusion of Language in Political Thought* (Occasional Paper 20, 1968), his Wincott Memorial Lecture, *Economic Freedom and Representative Government* (Occasional Paper 39, 1973), a collection of his writings with a new essay (assembled by Sudha Shenoy), *A Tiger by the Tail* (Hobart Paperback 4, 1972, Second Edition, 1978), an essay in *Verdict on Rent Control* (IEA Readings No. 7, 1972), *Full Employment at Any Price?* (Occasional Paper 45, 1975), *Choice in Currency: A Way to Stop Inflation* (Occasional Paper 48, 1976), and *Denationalisation of Money—The Argument Refined* (Hobart Paper 70, 1976, Second Edition, 1978).

# PART I

# Employment and Inflation

# 1980s Unemployment and the Unions

## F. A. HAYEK, CH

1. With an extensive division of labour, the aim of production cannot be the satisfaction of *known* demands; only market prices can inform the individual what to produce in his own and the general interest.

2. The pursuit of gain is the only way in which men can serve the requirements of others whom they do not know, and adjust their efforts to circumstances they cannot directly observe.

3. The prices paid for goods and services are not a 'just' reward for hard work but a *neutral* indicator of where resources require to be employed; social usefulness is not and cannot be apportioned according to any principles of justice.

4. The two alternatives to the market—collectivism and syndicalism—destroy not only wealth but freedom, whereas the market virtually eliminates coercion of men by other men.

5. The trade unions have become the biggest obstacle to raising the living standards of the working class as a whole; they are the chief cause of unemployment and the main reason for the decline of the British economy.

6. The present ability of any trade union to obtain better terms for its members rests chiefly on its legalised power to exploit other workers by preventing them from doing work they would like to do.

7. The *normal* cause of widespread unemployment is a discrepancy between the distribution of demand and that of production; its cure requires not an expansion of aggregate monetary demand but changes in relative wages to induce workers into jobs where they are needed.

8. Inflation may reduce unemployment in the short run, but its stimulative impact can be maintained only if it accelerates; in the longer run its accumulated effects are the cause of much greater unemployment.

9. No democratic government—at least in a highly industrialised country—can stay the course of a slow reduction of inflation over several years.

10. Britain remains paralysed by the consequences of the coercive powers irresponsibly conferred on the unions by law; there can be no salvation for her until these special privileges are revoked.

*Hobart Paper 87 (2nd Edition) is published (price £2·00) by*

**THE INSTITUTE OF ECONOMIC AFFAIRS**
**2 Lord North Street, Westminster**
**London SW1P 3LB    Telephone: 01-799 3745**

# IEA PUBLICATIONS

*Subscription Service*

An annual subscription is the most convenient way to obtain our publications. Every title we produce in all our regular series will be sent to you immediately on publication and without further charge, representing a substantial saving.

*Subscription rates**

*Britain:* £15.00 p.a. including postage.
£14.00 p.a. if paid by Banker's Order.
£10.00 p.a. teachers and students who pay *personally*.

*Europe and South America:* £20 or equivalent.

*Other countries:* Rates on application. In most countries subscriptions are handled by local agents.

*These rates are *not* available to companies or to institutions.

------------------------------------------------------------------

To: The Treasurer, Institute of Economic Affairs,
2 Lord North Street,
Westminster, London SW1P 3LB.

I should like to subscribe beginning ......................................
I enclose a cheque/postal order for:

☐ £15.00

☐ Please send me a Banker's Order form

☐ Please send me an Invoice

☐ £10.00 [I am a teacher/student at......................................]

Name ......................................................................

Address ...................................................................

............................................................................

Signed ................................................. Date..................

# 1980s Unemployment and the Unions

## F. A. HAYEK, CH

1. With an extensive division of labour, the aim of production cannot be the satisfaction of *known* demands; only market prices can inform the individual what to produce in his own and the general interest.

2. The pursuit of gain is the only way in which men can serve the requirements of others whom they do not know, and adjust their efforts to circumstances they cannot directly observe.

3. The prices paid for goods and services are not a 'just' reward for hard work but a *neutral* indicator of where resources require to be employed; social usefulness is not and cannot be apportioned according to any principles of justice.

4. The two alternatives to the market—collectivism and syndicalism—destroy not only wealth but freedom, whereas the market virtually eliminates coercion of men by other men.

5. The trade unions have become the biggest obstacle to raising the living standards of the working class as a whole; they are the chief cause of unemployment and the main reason for the decline of the British economy.

6. The present ability of any trade union to obtain better terms for its members rests chiefly on its legalised power to exploit other workers by preventing them from doing work they would like to do.

7. The *normal* cause of widespread unemployment is a discrepancy between the distribution of demand and that of production; its cure requires not an expansion of aggregate monetary demand but changes in relative wages to induce workers into jobs where they are needed.

8. Inflation may reduce unemployment in the short run, but its stimulative impact can be maintained only if it accelerates; in the longer run its accumulated effects are the cause of much greater unemployment.

9. No democratic government—at least in a highly industrialised country—can stay the course of a slow reduction of inflation over several years.

10. Britain remains paralysed by the consequences of the coercive powers irresponsibly conferred on the unions by law; there can be no salvation for her until these special privileges are revoked.

*Hobart Paper 87 (2nd Edition) is published (price £2·00) by*

 **THE INSTITUTE OF ECONOMIC AFFAIRS**
**2 Lord North Street, Westminster**
**London SW1P 3LB   Telephone: 01-799 3745**

# IEA PUBLICATIONS

*Subscription Service*

An annual subscription is the most convenient way to obtain our publications. Every title we produce in all our regular series will be sent to you immediately on publication and without further charge, representing a substantial saving.

*Subscription rates**

*Britain:* £15.00 p.a. including postage.
£14.00 p.a. if paid by Banker's Order.
£10.00 p.a. teachers and students who pay *personally.*

*Europe and South America:* £20 or equivalent.

*Other countries:* Rates on application. In most countries subscriptions are handled by local agents.

*These rates are *not* available to companies or to institutions.

------------------------------------------------------------------

To: The Treasurer, Institute of Economic Affairs,
2 Lord North Street,
Westminster, London SW1P 3LB.

I should like to subscribe beginning .........................................
I enclose a cheque/postal order for:

☐ £15.00

☐ Please send me a Banker's Order form

☐ Please send me an Invoice

☐ £10.00 [I am a teacher/student at.....................................]

Name .................................................................................

Address ..............................................................................

........................................................................

Signed ................................................ Date ..................

British sentiments on unemployment and opinions on the effective remedies for it have been shaped by a unique historical experience that has given rise to a persuasive but false theory which for a generation has dominated discussion. The unique situation was created by Britain's decision after World War I to return to gold at the pre-war parity. This was a very honest decision for the banker of the world which may have seemed necessary to preserve that position. But it proved a very unwise decision, at least when it was decided to achieve this result slowly and gradually. It had certainly not been understood what it would mean to drag out over a decade the process of adapting internal prices and wages to world levels.

The United States had set a different example. There, in the short period of less than a year, from the middle of 1920 to the middle of 1921, monetary policy succeeded in bringing wholesale prices down by 44 per cent, thereby restoring the value of the dollar to its pre-war level. The suffering during this period was great, but the foundations for a speedy resumption of prosperity were laid: in the following two years industrial production rose by 63 per cent and the national product by 23 per cent.

*Painful consequences for Britain of restoring the gold standard in 1925*

Britain chose otherwise. Though the clear determination of the Government to restore the gold standard made it possible to do so as early as 1925, internal prices and wages were then still far from being adapted to the international level. To maintain this parity, a slow and highly painful process of deflation was initiated, bringing lasting and extensive unemployment, to be abandoned only when it became intolerable when intensified by the world crisis of 1931—but, I am still inclined to believe, just at a time when the aim of that painful struggle had been nearly achieved.

During this period, which fashioned the outlook of the next generation, Britain found herself in the exceptional position, as an effect of the policy pursued, that all wages in the export industries on which the people depended for their livelihood were too high. In these conditions it was indeed approximately

[15]

true that a rise of total demand would have been an effective way of lastingly removing most of the unemployment. The idea that general employment was determined by the relation of aggregate demand for final products prevailing in a given country (or monetary community) to the costs of the supply of goods, true enough under the special conditions of the time, unfortunately then came to dominate the monetary theory of the following generations and was applied in wholly different circumstances in which it became very misleading.

While the possibility of selling different quantities of *one* commodity depends of course on the magnitude of the demand for it, the possibility of selling a collection of a wide variety of different commodities is not in any simple manner related to the sum of the demands for all of them together. If the composition (or distribution) of the demand for the various products is very different from that of their supply, no magnitude of total demand will assure that the market is cleared. The wider the difference between the composition of the demand and that of the supply, the more the achievement of a correspondence between the whole of demand and the whole of supply can be brought about *only* by a change in the relative quantities, *and* this, in turn, only by a change in the relative prices of the different products and services, including wages. This is a major problem even if we think only of the possible discrepancies of demand and supply of all the final products— or what the economists are in the habit of calling the 'horizontal' dimension of the structure of production. But the complexity becomes immense when we include in our considerations the fact that all that is done at any one time does not serve the wants of one single point of time but the wants of many future dates, and that at each of these 'stages' varying expectations of the future will cause independent and different fluctuations of demand and supply. Once one comprehends this truth, the belief that a management of aggregate final demand can secure lasting full employment must look very naïve; and it seems inevitable that a policy based on such a crude conception would be bound in the end to make things worse rather than better.

*Closeness of match of distribution of demand and supply determines aggregate employment*

The rate of general employment thus depends on the degree of correspondence between the distribution of demand and

[16]

the distribution of supply. And it is the distribution of supply which must adapt itself to the distribution of demand—even more than elsewhere in a country largely dependent on exports, over the demands for which it has no control. Aggregate demand may well exceed the aggregate price of all goods and services offered, yet this will not create full employment if in the sectors in which demand exceeds supply the already employed obstruct the entry of additional workers by claiming all the surplus as gain for themselves. Nor will people move out of the sector with a relative deficiency of demand unless it is clear that they cannot all hope to continue to earn there the wages they used to receive.

The disappearance of *some* employment opportunities is a necessary feature not only of any progressive but even of a stationary economy operating in a changing environment. If every firm were forced to continue employing its whole staff at the terms originally agreed upon, it would indeed have to continue until it went down with all hands, dragging down even those for whom it might have continued to provide a living. This appears to happen in Japan, where security of job while the firm lasts seems to produce a frequency of bankruptcies unequalled elsewhere.

One of the most vivid memories of my many defeats is of a discussion at the London Economic Club some 30 or 40 years ago when I let myself be silenced by a retort of Mr R. G. Hawtrey, as he then was, to the effect that what I apparently wanted were 'bigger and better bankruptcies'. I am not sure that Britain would not have attained a stronger position if she had allowed this. People seem to forget that the bankruptcy of a company need not mean the disappearance of its productive *equipment* but merely the replacement of an unsuccessful *management* by a new one.

Jobs are from the beginning a product of the market. In the long run only the market can provide ever new jobs which in a changing world must be constantly found to maintain all those whom the market in the first instance enabled to live by selling their labour. The numbers which can be maintained by transferring to them income taken by taxation from others is limited. And this is what has to be done to keep people employed who are given a larger share of the product than they contribute. Nobody can claim a moral right to employment at a particular wage, unless there is opportunity profitably to

[17]

employ him at such wages. The problem today is that access to such employment is denied to him by the monopolistic organisations of his fellows. All opportunities for employment are a creation of the market and the classical ideal of 'full employment at high wages' (J. S. Mill) can be achieved only by a functioning market on which the wages offered for different kinds of work tell the worker where, in the circumstances of the moment, he can make the largest contribution to the social product.

### Trade unions obstruct adaptation of relative prices (especially wages) to the distribution of demand

It is the continuous change of *relative* market prices and particularly wages which alone can bring about that steady adjustment of the proportions of the different efforts to the distribution of demand, and thus a steady flow of the stream of products. It is this incessant adaptation of relative wages to the ever-changing magnitudes, at which in each sector demand will equal supply, which the trade unions have set out to inhibit. Wages are no longer to be determined by demand and supply but by alleged considerations of justice, which means in effect not only simply custom and tradition but increasingly sheer power. The market is thereby deprived of the function of guiding labour to where it can be sold.

### Unemployment inevitable

It is inevitable that this obstruction of the market should produce extensive unemployment. And if it had not been for a scapegoat to which responsibility could be diverted, even the members of the trade unions would long ago have been forced to admit that the policies of the unions were, under normal conditions, the sole cause of extensive lasting unemployment as well as the chief obstacle to a faster rise of the income of the workers. This scapegoat, raised by the persuasive voice of Lord Keynes to the position of a generally accepted dogma, was 'aggregate demand' depending on the supply of money.

The scapegoat possessed a certain plausibility because of the unique experience of Britain half a century ago, when it was indeed true that policy had created a situation where the *general* wage level of Britain was too high and the unemployment could have been cured by increasing aggregate demand by lowering the external value of sterling.

It was a great historical misfortune that this special experience had directed attention to a more painless remedy which, however, could be employed effectively only in the special circumstances of that time. This view, however, pleased the traditional sympathy of the British public with the efforts of the trade unions by relieving them of the responsibility for the bad effects of their efforts. Most people were happy to learn that government had the power, and therefore the exclusive responsibility, to secure full employment. But this release of the trade unions from the responsibility for the effects of their actions also removed the chief restraint on the abuse of their power.

In post-World War II Britain it was no longer the general level of money wages which was too high. It should indeed have been higher with a free market for labour in which monopolistic groups could not deprive others of their chances. It is the wages maintained by the closed shops whose barriers prevented the rest from earning as much as they might have done which keeps the productivity of the majority of British workers low. Once the opportunity to earn more in a particular trade becomes the exclusive property of those already employed there, successes of individual enterprises are likely to be taken out by its present staff in the form of higher wages rather than leading to additional employment.

*Inflation, employment and trade unions: Britain, 1980s*

The problem of inflation, the problem of employment, and the problem of the excessive power of the trade unions have become inseparable in present-day Britain. Although seen as a problem of economic cause and effect, there is no such thing as 'cost-push inflation'. The only effect of an excessive rise of wages (or of the price of anything else) would be that what is offered cannot be sold. *Politically* the problem of trade union power is the primary problem because, so long as government has the control of the supply of money, it will be forced to resort to the palliative of inflation which temporarily disguises the effects of a rise of wages on employment but leads to cumulative arrears of omitted adaptations which merely store up later trouble.

[19]

Indeed, the reliance on monetary expansion as a cure for unemployment would not be so harmful if it were merely a temporary palliative, ineffective to cure the underlying causes. What makes it so dangerous is that it actually and continuously makes matters worse. It not only preserves the existing but leads to a continuous accumulation of further misdirections of efforts which ought to have been currently corrected. *Monetary demand not based on real earnings can last only so long as the additions to the supply of money grow.*

*The palliative (monetary expansion) is the pernicious poison (inflation)*

But the palliative, so tempting to the politician, proves to be a poison, and, because it is habit-forming, pernicious even in the smallest doses. Although one hesitates to use this worn metaphor, the whole situation as well as the moral issues involved are much the same as those presented by some habit-forming drug which can produce a passing state of euphoria necessarily followed by withdrawal symptoms of severe depression. People who advocate its use as a stimulant, except in an acute political emergency, are simply quacks. There is only one important difference between the individual and the political problem: while a human patient may under medical direction last through a protracted treatment, no political community will long bear the suffering connected with such a slow cure.

Surprising as it may seem, these after-effects of inflation have been much neglected by economists. They were mainly concerned with its *current* effects on the relation between debtors and creditors, with the suffering of all those whose income was determined by long-term contracts, including wage earners, and with the general injustice of the arbitrary redistribution of incomes which inflation causes while it proceeds. This is the effect which everybody soon learns to see, the source of general complaint, and it seems of all that most economists are aware of who think exclusively in terms of the effects of *average* prices. For them inflation is an evil which can be slowly and gradually reduced, and in the fight against which every slowing-down of the rate of inflation is a gain. But the chief penalty for past inflation must be paid so long as it is being reduced and for some time after it has been stopped.

To reduce present unemployment by inflation always becomes the cause of greater unemployment later, because the effect of making possible a postponement of necessary adaptations is cumulative and in the course of time creates an amount of maladjustment which nobody is prepared to face. The artificial demand brought about by increasing the amount of money is simply misleading: it attracts workers into employments which cannot be maintained except by *accelerating* inflation. The crucial point that must be recognised is that it is not the *size* of total demand but the *distribution* of demand which decides whether a level of employment can be maintained. There is no substitute for a flexible wage structure. The vain search for a palliative while preserving the unions' strength is the chief source of Britain's economic decline.

If in the short run inflation reduces unemployment, in the long run its accumulated effects will make much more unemployment inevitable than it temporarily reduced. To see this result it is necessary to understand fully the process through which for a time a general rise of prices can make activities profitable which are bound to fail as soon as inflation *ceases to accelerate*. This is particularly important in order to refute the uncomprehending or malicious allegations in Britain that unemployment is now deliberately created as a means to stop inflation. Unemployment has been made inevitable by past inflation; it has merely been *postponed* by accelerating inflation. *But those responsible for the present unemployment are those who caused the inflation, not those who are trying to stop it.* To postpone this any further could merely make the eventual outcome worse. It is simply not within human power to postpone the evil day indefinitely. An inflationary boom must collapse sooner or later with the consequence of large unemployment.

Inflation cannot be accelerated indefinitely. Though even a fairly rapidly depreciating money will still serve as a means of calculation, it ceases to do so once the rate of depreciation exceeds a certain speed. When prices begin to double every year, and then every month or every week, and finally every day (and I have seen this happen), the money in terms of which this occurs is discarded by the public. But once acceleration of inflation is accepted as indispensable to maintain employment, this point must eventually be reached. What then puts an end to it is that people refuse to sell for this sort of money and other means of exchange take the place of those which government provided.

[21]

## Repressed inflation via price controls or incomes policy more damaging than open inflation

The expedient which is likely to postpone this inevitable ultimate outcome for a long time at the price of even more damage done is widely thought to be price controls. I have been preaching on this topic for years that if anything is worse than an open inflation it is a repressed inflation, an increase in the quantity of money which proceeds but by legal price-fixing is prevented from showing any effects on prices. If an *open* inflation severely distorts the steering function of the market, a *repressed* inflation completely suspends it. Price fixing or an incomes policy means no less than a transition from a market economy to a planned economy with all its inevitable consequences.

## Britain in the 1980s

The acute problem for Britain at present is still whether to stop inflation dead instantly or to protract the process of reducing it over months or years, and the answer to this must depend on our insight about how inflation operates which we had begun discussing. The crucial point was that it can preserve its stimulating effect only so long as it accelerates, and that as soon as it ceases to accelerate all the misdirections of production which it has caused will show themselves. In practice, terminating the acceleration of inflation, and even more gradually reducing the rate of inflation, must have an effect very similar to deflation. It will cause the same widespread disappointment of expectations and force the suspension of activities which had been kept going by prices turning out to be higher than they ought to have been.

The difference between the two phenomena is that, while we can always prevent deflation, once we have embarked on an accelerating inflation we will sooner or later be forced to stop it, if not earlier at least when people refuse to hold or even accept the money with its fast-dwindling buying power. And since any inflation, however modest at first, can help employment only so long as it accelerates, adopted as a means of reducing unemployment, it will do so for any length of time only while it accelerates.

### *'Mild' steady inflation cannot help—it can lead only to outright inflation*

That inflation at a constant rate soon ceases to have any stimulating effect, and in the end merely leaves us with a backlog of delayed adaptations, is the conclusive argument against the 'mild' inflation represented as beneficial even in standard economics textbooks. Those who advocate, or even are merely prepared to tolerate, mild inflation are inevitably driven to support more and more inflation. Nor is anything gained by merely reducing inflation to a 'reasonable' rate. *Inflation must be stopped dead*, because the trouble about it is precisely that its stimulating effect can be preserved only by accelerating it. Once a given rate of inflation is generally *expected*, it no longer stimulates but only continues to preserve some of the misdirections of efforts it has caused. But so long as it is believed that general employment is determined by a monetary policy which in the long run will only make matters worse, to begin with a mild expansion will invariably lead to outright inflation.

### *Slowly falling inflation with high unemployment likely to fail in an industrial democracy*

Considered as a purely technical problem of monetary policy, we have of course the choice whether we wish to reduce inflation slowly and gradually or instantly. In neither case can we escape causing thereby for a time extensive unemployment. This has been made inescapable by what has happened earlier. For a short time the amount of unemployment may be even higher when the termination of inflation is effected quickly than it will ever be during the long process of a gradual return. Politically, however, we may not be able to choose. A drastic cut, however painful, will be tolerable and would be patiently submitted to if there were hope of recovery in the near future. I do not believe that any democratic government can stay the course of a slow reduction of inflation over years—at least not in a highly industrialised country. Even 20 per cent unemployment would probably be borne for six months if there existed confidence that it would be over at the end of such a period. But I doubt whether any government could persist for two or three years in a policy that meant 10 per cent unemployment for most of that period. Such efforts will prove vain and the

[23]

suffering wasted if public opinion makes it necessary to break it off before the desired result has been achieved.

I am of course fully aware of the immense problem of public finance involved in being suddenly deprived of the means for covering a budget deficit which the creation of money has provided. But, however difficult, it can be solved and must be solved if the last chance of avoiding a final collapse of the British economy is to be taken. Though a real balancing of the budget requires a period of some length, the necessary borrowing does not have to be based on increasing the circulation of sterling.

At a time when the ordinary citizen is in desperate difficulty to find an opportunity for stable investments of his savings, a large government loan in terms of a new stable unit could be raised very cheaply and bring into the government's pockets funds which the citizen would probably otherwise spend. As I have suggested on another occasion (*The Times*, 13 June 1980):

'Large amounts could probably be raised at perhaps 3 or even 2½ per cent if a public which no longer knows what to do with its savings were offered such an opportunity. It seems to me that the British government, perhaps undeservedly, still enjoys a reputation for honesty which may make an experiment of this sort a great success. The "solids", in terms of which the loan would be issued, would have to be defined as, and be redeemable in, so much of a bundle of other currencies as would at the time be required to buy on the world market a "basket" of a wide range of internationally traded raw materials in precisely stated quantitative combinations. Ultimately the unit might become, if necessary, the basis of a new British currency.'

# PART II

# The Telecommunications System of the Market

Many people seem to believe that freedom consists of being able to do whatever they like and still enjoy all the benefits of an advanced society in which they must co-operate with others. But modern society, which rests on a far-ranging division of labour, could not prosper—or even survive for long —if it allowed the mass of its members that kind of freedom. Its relative opulence requires all of us to observe an impersonal discipline. More than once in our lifetimes, some of us have to do things we may dislike—changing our jobs, our homes or our neighbourhoods, or accepting a smaller income than we had come to expect, and so on. And all this is hard to bear because it seems the consequence of causes and events a long way off about which we know nothing: a change of habit in another industry or a technical invention in another country. Nobody is morally entitled to claim a share in the wealth which such a society produces unless he is prepared to obey the discipline of other people's wants or other countries' production methods that are ultimately the sources of our wealth.

*Producing the desired commodity in the most economic way at the required time is what counts, not 'working hard'*

With an extensive 'division of labour', in which we all specialise in producing goods and services, we must be ready to change the nature or direction of our efforts, or accept less than our accustomed income, in response to unforeseen circumstances and unforeseen changes in them. All *economic* problems are caused by *unforeseen* events. Otherwise we could simply continue doing what we decided long ago without ever having to change our work, our industry, or our homes.

In an economic system whose productivity, in this sense of producing what others want, rests on a worldwide division of labour and specialisation, the size of the national product will depend not on individuals 'working hard' but on making the 'right' (desired) things in the 'right' (most economic) manner and at the 'right' time (required by the consumer in the market which may be hundreds or thousands of miles away in other continents). The way in which at any one time the individual

[27]

can make the largest contribution to the product of society and thereby maximise his share of that product in the form of wages, salaries, etc., will depend on the new opportunities opening up from day to day for thousands of workers in other occupations with whom he co-operates in producing something —often without knowing it—or from consumers whose demands he serves—usually without knowing them at all.

### Market prices convey information to change course

Each individual can rarely know the conditions which make it desirable, for him as well as for others, to do one thing rather than another, or to do it in one way rather than another. *It is only through the prices he finds in the market that he can learn what to do and how.* Only they, constantly and unmistakably, can inform him what goods or services he ought to produce in his own interest as well as the general interest of his community or country as a whole. The 'signal' which warns him that he must alter the direction or nature of his effort is frequently the discovery that he can no longer sell the fruits of his effort at prices which leave a surplus over costs. This signalling apparatus works as much for the employed worker as for the professional or business man.

In a free society nobody can compel another person to continue in his job. And, in most instances, he will have alternatives open to him. Yet signals which nobody has deliberately set will often inform him that what he has been producing, and what he would readily continue producing as industriously as before, will no longer earn him as much as it has done, or as much as he could earn elsewhere in another job or industry. The signals may thus tell him that he may even earn nothing at all if he continues in what he has been producing. All the conscientious devotion in the world will earn nothing for the workers making Triumph motor-cycles if the motor-cyclists in Britain and overseas want other cycles.

For anyone earning his living in the market, which means most of us, the most valuable contribution he can make at any time will depend on thousands of continually changing conditions of which he can have no direct knowledge. It is nevertheless possible for him to make whatever decisions are most advantageous both to himself and the community at large because the open market conveys to him, through its prices, the information he requires to make the right decisions and choices. The prices are thus the indispensable signals that communicate to him the effects of events with which he cannot himself be directly acquainted.

### Division of labour and technology constantly changing

The division of labour among individuals, firms or countries is not once-for-all but a complex, balanced structure which must continuously change to perform its function. It is a fatal mistake, frequently made by engineers or other natural scientists, to imagine there are long-lasting, technically-determined production methods which are superior to all others, and that these make it possible to continue the use of the factors in rigid quantitative proportions. It is not 'good technology' which determines productivity but the right choice among the many technologies available. This is an economic, not a technological, problem.

The vast increase in output and living standards made possible by the wide-ranging division of labour in the modern Western world is chiefly the result of goods and services being produced by those best able to do so and of their using the means of production which sacrifice as little as necessary of other goods or services that could have been produced with the resources, so that their 'opportunity costs' are minimised.

It is solely through the effects which unknown, remote events have on prices that the individual employer, producer or dealer can take account of changes in the conditions in which raw materials are produced, in the demand for some final products for which his contribution is needed, or in technology. Such events will sometimes affect only indirectly, and at many removes, the activity with which he is directly concerned. And that indirect route takes the form of substituting objects which have become relatively cheaper for other objects which have become relatively dearer.

### Efficient use of resources guided unconsciously by remote control of millions unknown to one another

All effort to make the best use of available resources is thus guided by a sort of remote control. The signals which inform individuals what they should produce are not deliberately set by anyone. They are the joint result of all the individuals

[29]

using, for their own purposes, the detailed information they know. And the prices which guide them are formed by incorporating all the effects of their demands and supplies.

What prices tell everybody is the rate at which (or the proportion in which) other people can (for their own purposes) substitute a quantity of one commodity for quantities of another. If any commodity is worth more to an individual relatively to another commodity than the current market rate, he can exchange it to the extent he desires. In doing so he will affect the price and contribute his mite of information to the signals. It is thus the consequent tendency towards similarity of all internal rates of substitution of different persons (counting all the costs of passing goods from one person's control to another's) which secures the most efficient use of resources. This result is achieved through using the knowledge possessed by the participants in the market, whether they know one another or not. Each individual can thus produce his output at the least cost in terms of the products that others, in consequence, will lack and want.

### *Far-ranging division of labour made possible only by self-steering market process*

It is as if all participants in the market had before them the current results of a giant computer into which each of them, in the light of the available data, could feed his own offers and demands by pressing a few buttons. But such a computer would be helpful only if everybody had full access to it all the time and was committed to buy and sell what was on offer or in demand, so that nobody could manipulate the market by false information. In practice, the real market attains only an approximation to this ideal, but it is as close an approximation as we can achieve with the imperfect information available.

Although Adam Smith told us 200 years ago in *The Wealth of Nations* that

> 'this division of labour, from which so many advantages are derived, is not originally the effect of any human wisdom, which foresees and intends the general opulence to which it gives occasion',

most people, especially 'social engineers', still conceive of it as something designed, or at least designable, such as the division of labour within a single factory. Smith himself contributed to

[30]

this misconception by deriving his most famous illustration from the organisation of pin-making by several workers each doing a specialised job. Adam Smith clearly understood but did not fully explain that the division of labour among many people who know nothing of each other is made possible only by the market. It would develop through such a self-steering process *only because it uses more information than any directing agency could ever possess.*

Modern societies can produce as much as they do because everybody is informed by market prices of the highest costs at which it is worthwhile producing any particular commodity or service. And each producer can find out how and whether he can produce at such costs only because he can calculate his own costs in comparison with the prices that reflect all the other uses to which the resources he employs might be put.

### *Production for satisfaction of known wants impossible with extensive division of labour*

Because the division of labour is among millions of people who do not even know of the existence of most of the others for whom and in co-operation with whom they unwittingly work, their aim becomes impersonal and, in a sense, abstract. The aim of the efforts of all can no longer be the satisfaction of *known* demands, for they have no knowledge of the subsequent use of their products. The aim must therefore become solely the yield from the sale of their products on the market. To obtain such a return, each individual must seek to meet the demands of other people at least as cheaply as anyone else does. Everybody's effort must thus be directed at producing goods and services at costs as much as possible *below* current prices. The *difference* between costs and returns, which we disdainfully call 'gain' or 'profit', thus becomes the true measure of the social usefulness to others of our efforts. And production at a loss, when costs exceed the yield, becomes an offence against the best use of resources. And this is especially true when it means, as it so often does, that someone else's resources are being misused.

The difference between obeying and not obeying the signals of prices and costs is, therefore, the difference between productive and unproductive effort—between effort which increases and effort which diminishes the national product. We might also call it the difference between socially beneficial and anti-social activities.

### Market prices are not perfect but the best available

This analysis is not substantially modified by the undeniable truth that even the most perfect market prices do not take into account *all* the circumstances we would wish—often described as 'external' conditions. But where we have to adapt production to many more events than we can be aware of, a signal which takes account of most of them is better than none. Travellers do not throw away the map of a strange country they have to cross because they find it is not wholly accurate.

### Only free prices send reliable signals; administered prices mislead

Only prices at which everyone is free to buy and sell as much as he wants and his means allow can operate as reliable guides. Only if all owners or users of goods can take part in the dealings will all requirements and all opportunities be taken into account. Prices fixed by political authority, or prices influenced by controls on demand and supply—such as rationing, subsidies, special taxes—do not guide in the right direction but generally mislead because they distort the information about supply and consumer demand and, moreover, add a political element that has little to do with reflecting technical possibilities or satisfying consumers.

### Monopoly prices can be made least harmful by maintaining competition

Prices may, for a time, be fixed by a monopolist who owes his position not to privilege conferred upon him by government, but to his superior efficiency which nobody else can equal. Consumers have scarcely any right to force such a producer to do as well as he can if he is already doing better than anybody else in his industry. We can only make it necessary for all producers to do at least as well as those producers whom we pay the same price for the same product. But the use of power to restrict competition, or to deny new producers access to a market in order to keep prices at a desired figure, will prevent some relevant information about conditions of supply from being taken into account.

Contrary to a widespread belief, unless it is sheltered from competition by government protection, a big business has no more power than anyone else to fix prices arbitrarily. It is subject to the same disciplines of supply and demand. And if such a firm mistakes the signals, it will, fortunately, fail—at least so long as government does not bail it out, as has recently happened in Britain.

### Pursuit of gain creates indirect incentives to serve others

The pursuit of gain is thus the only way in which men can serve the requirements of others whom they do not know, and adjust their efforts to circumstances they cannot directly observe. The pursuit of gain is held in bad repute, because it does not have as its aim the *visible* benefit of others and may be successfully guided by purely selfish motives. Yet the source of the strength of the market order is that it uses the immediate concerns of individuals to make them serve needs that are more important than they can know. It is not because a man's aims are 'selfish' but because they are his own that he can contribute, through his free decisions guided by the signals of prices, more to the welfare of others than if that were his direct goal. His efforts may not be the most beneficial to his *immediate* neighbours—and for that reason may not make him popular among them—but he will thus serve society at large much better than he could in any other way.

### Discovering relevant information only through competition: the telecommunications of the market

In this manner, the market not only matches millions of separate efforts to one another so that, on the whole, the demand for a commodity or a service (including, of course, labour) will approximately correspond to its supply at market prices. The market also obliges and enables all participants— buyers and sellers—to obtain a given output from a *minimum* of resources available to them. Put another way, it induces everyone to obtain from a given input of resources as *large* a proportion of the social product as possible.

They can do this only because they can calculate, in terms of the costs of labour, capital, etc., the cheapest way of producing what they can expect to sell at a known price. Without prices determined by competition, in which the variegated knowledge and requirements of millions are reflected, effective calculation

[33]

would be impossible. Prices administered by central authority, as in Russia and Poland (or Britain and the USA), on the other hand, which must be based on much less information than that reflected by competitive prices, are often likely to show a surplus on activities which are socially loss-making, or *vice-versa*. They therefore cause massive misdirection of human and natural resources in producing commodities or services that the people do not want.

With given competitive prices, each participant in the productive process can attempt to produce, from any given quantity of resources, as large an output as can be achieved. The use of the existing but dispersed information about detailed circumstances, where nobody can always know who possesses that information, requires competition as the process of *selection* which finds ('discovers') the possessor of the relevant information. Only the telecommunications system of the market can enable the participants to discover which method of production is cheapest, in terms of the other commodities or services we should like, and for which the resources could have been used.

### British 'anti-economics' in the use of productive resources

All economising in production means that we use less of one resource and more of another: materials, energy, equipment or human labour. This process always requires constant adaptation to new circumstances since, as I have argued, all economic problems are problems of adaptation to *unknown* and *unforeseen* change.

Producing cheaply means using as few resources as possible, measured in terms of the rates (prices) at which different products could be substituted for each other in their various uses. And reducing costs means setting free resources which could produce more elsewhere. In any particular instance, the primary aim must therefore always be to use as few resources as possible for a given output. Only as a result of producing as cheaply as possible will people have income to spare to pay for the work of others. The secret of productivity which makes it possible to employ many at high wages is for each producer to do his job with the use of as few resources as possible.

In Britain the unfortunate experience of long periods of unemployment, due to exceptional historical, and not necessarily recurring, circumstances, has made the people forget this

[34]

fundamental truth. It has led them to behave as if the direct aim of economic activity were to use as *many* resources as possible. It has come to be thought in Britain that a prime task of economic policy was the protection of *existing* jobs. This fundamental reversal of the truth has developed into a sort of anti-economics which has misrepresented the chief social goal to be the use of as *large* a quantity of resources as possible.

### Job creation and credit expansion are the creators of unemployment

This view of economic policy finds support in the statistical nonsense, common in Western countries since the war, of measuring the social product in terms of costs. In a country like Britain, heavily dependent on selling its products to the rest of the world, this whole approach must have the opposite effect on employment from the one intended. Government efforts—which are politically unavoidable under the prevailing form of unlimited democracy—to enable workers to retain employment which has become unprofitable at existing wages only increase the backlog of necessary job adjustments. Sooner or later, the backlog must lead to unemployment. And the longer it is deferred, the more the unemployment.

Attempts in recent years to achieve full employment through credit expansion—to draw workers into jobs which can last only so long as inflation progressively accelerates—have, moreover, markedly exacerbated that effect. To consider the manipulation of aggregate demand as a means of securing an efficient use of resources, i.e. of directing them where they ought to be used, is anti-economics. Britain has been brought to her present plight, not because of the lack of skill or industry of the individual worker, but because government and labour organisations, in order to appease groups of workers, have tried to relieve them of the necessity for adjustments by removing the inducements (and rewards) of changing their jobs.

### Competition essential for controlling costs

In the absence of a competitive market in which freely-determined prices inform all producers of the socially cheapest way of producing commodities or services, and at what prices other producers can supply them, costs easily get out of control. Without the help of such information-creating prices, managers, who tend to be concerned chiefly about the physical process of production and are perhaps fascinated by the beauty of the technique employed, can quickly let the outlay on production rise to double what it would otherwise be. This lack of market information means that twice as much could have been produced from the amount of resources consumed.

Neither does this reduction of output below potential measure the whole loss a country may suffer as a result of a distorted price structure. For a firm or country producing for sale in competition with others, costs higher than the necessary level by perhaps only one or two per cent may mean the complete loss of the business, and therefore of the whole income derived from it.

It is by this constant pressure that competition leaves buyers and sellers in the market no choice but to make use of *all* the available possibilities in combining resources to avoid unnecessary costs. The absence of this pressure on producers and suppliers is certain to raise costs unnecessarily. A country which lives on imports, like Britain, may thus become unable to pay for them.

# Three Options for Policy

There are three attitudes which organised power can take towards the extensive division of labour required in an advanced society.

### Refine the legal framework—especially to catch 'externalities'

First, legislation and government may cultivate the market—as they did for a long time, without really understanding its requirements. Through trial and error they could gradually develop the framework of private and criminal law required by the system of private property. Assisted by a better understanding of the working of the market, we might continue these efforts to improve the legal framework where we find it defective. In particular, the current delimitation of property rights may not catch the 'external' effects that at present are not adequately taken into account by prices.

### Emulate or 'correct' the market by central planning—but impossible to agree on objectives

Secondly, the public authority might try to emulate the market's allocation of resources by a system of central direction. Such a system of collectivist economic planning has, for a long time, exercised intense fascination for many people. It was thought the way to achieve not only a more efficient economic process but also a more just distribution of incomes. But the initial hope soon had to be abandoned when it was realised that no planning authority could ever use all the information about detailed circumstances that is dispersed among hundreds of thousands of individuals, to anything like the extent to which the market uses it day by day.

Even attempts to 'correct' the prices set by the market, through the intervention of authority, must founder. It is impossible sensibly to correct a signal (price) that conveys information on the combined effects of changes in supply and demand of which the authority itself does not know. The hope of achieving a more just distribution of incomes in this way is doomed to disappointment. Not only could few people agree on what a just distribution of incomes would be. Even more serious, any attempt to reward people according to some principle of merit or 'need', instead of according to the value of their services to their fellows (which may be very different), would make voluntary collaboration in the efficient use of resources impossible.

*Syndicalist or corporativist organisation of interest groups is anti-social*
Thirdly, there is the syndicalist-corporativist response. This amounts to a systematic obstruction and sabotage of price determination through the competitive market by organised sectional interests that are permitted to use power and coercion to maintain their monopoly. In almost all instances their aim is to secure for their members a larger share of the social income. Yet, at the same time, the restrictive methods they employ reduce that total. They are therefore anti-social in the only proper sense of the word. By bringing about a larger loss to the community, they secure for themselves a smaller gain. Yet these practices are today common in Britain among groups whose membership probably adds up to a large proportion of the population.

*Central direction and monopoly domination combined in futile 'incomes policies'*
It is scarcely an exaggeration to say that, while we still owe our current living standards chiefly to the operation of an increasingly mutilated market system, economic policy is guided almost entirely by a combination of the two views whose object is to destroy the market: the planning ambitions of doctrinaire socialist intellectuals and the restrictionism of trade unions and trade associations. This paradox continues although, until the most recent times, the market order has again and again produced the outstanding successes around the world, while no attempt to determine the division of labour by either central planning or monopolies has ever succeeded. What today is called an 'incomes policy' is merely an attempt to reconcile these two policies, equally hostile to the market, in a futile endeavour to combat inflation. Every effort in this direction constitutes a new blow at the competitiveness of British industry.

*The market as liberator: minimises coercion and fraud*
From a human viewpoint the perhaps most profound advantage of the market over alternative methods of directing the use of

[40]

resources is that it virtually eliminates the use of force and the coercion of men by other men. This result is in marked contrast to the inexorable subjection to superiors which is an essential and indispensable ingredient of socialism and monopoly.

It may be true that, in the last century in communities with only a single factory or mine, the local manager could exercise an almost dictatorial power over the workers. The distance-annihilating increase in mobility occasioned by modern communications, and particularly by the motor-car, has removed this subjection to monopoly. But, in general, probably never in the whole of recorded history was the exercise of arbitrary power and the personal subjection of human beings to the power of others reduced so much as during the second half of the last century—that period which we like to call, contemptuously and misleadingly, the age of *laissez-faire*. Compared with the feudalism of the preceding centuries, it gave a degree of individual freedom to the working population previously unknown in the history of civilisation. During that period, any citizen of the Western industrial countries could proudly claim he was not irrevocably subject to any man's orders.

### Collectivism and syndicalism destroy freedom and wealth

The two alternative systems, on the other hand, require a return to coercion without rule. They demand personal submission to a superior to whom a man is assigned, or to dependence on an organised group of special interests whose pleasure determines whether a man is allowed to earn his living in a particular way. The two systems are bound to destroy not only personal freedom but also the wealth on which the group members base their demands. This is so because that wealth is founded on the use of widely dispersed information, which is created only if everybody is allowed to employ his own knowledge for his own purposes and if prices are formed in a free market so as to convey to him the information he requires to fit his efforts into the general pattern of economic activity.

### The market rewards what should be done to satisfy consumer preferences, not what is done by producers

It is this highly sensitive, though somewhat delicate, instrument that makes possible an efficient use of resources. But the would-be reformers want to destroy it because they will not understand that something which has never been deliberately designed but has grown through a process of selective evolution can achieve more than rational direction ever could. Their main complaint is that the market order distributes benefits with little regard to justice. In a sense, this is true and even necessary, because the prices paid for different individuals' services are not designed as a reward for what they have done but function as an indicator of what they ought to do. The prices paid for services are not a 'just' reward for effort but a neutral indicator of where they require to be applied.

### Planned efficiency could be no more 'just' than market efficiency

The director of a planned society who wanted to secure an efficient use of resources, and to use wages as an inducement to workers to go where they were required, could be no more just than the market. A steering mechanism to achieve adaptation to unforeseen changes cannot be 'just'. Adaptation to an unknown number of unforeseen events, which in their totality cannot be known to anybody but to which all submit under the same abstract rules, cannot be designed. It is therefore incapable of being 'just'.

*Social usefulness is not and cannot be apportioned according to any principles of justice.* If we want to induce people to offer what will produce the largest contribution to the requirements of others, we must allow them to earn incomes that correspond to their performance, rather than to their merits or needs.

### Marx stood reality on its head: the labour value error of classical economics

The guide rôle of prices, which Adam Smith clearly understood, was later obscured by the labour theory of value of Ricardo, the two Mills and Karl Marx. They inverted the true causal relationship. Instead of showing that prices informed producers how much labour it was worth putting into an object, they taught that the value of a product was determined by the labour invested in it. It is this inversion of the true functional relationship of value (informing people how much cost it is worthwhile incurring to produce things) into the belief that values are a result of people having invested costs in producing them that incapacitates Marxists from ever understanding the function of the market.

This error of classical theory, from which British (or, at least, Cambridge) economics never quite recovered, bears some responsibility for the recent economic decline of Britain. To reverse it requires recognition of the market as a communication system which achieves something that no other known system could possibly achieve.

## The harmful legacy of our moral instincts

Our inherited moral feelings constitute the stubborn obstacle to the moral approval of the market system to which we owe our wealth. They demand that we consciously aim at benefiting other known persons; in contrast, the beneficial effects of our efforts on other people in the market society are mostly unknown to us and cannot guide us. In order to do most good the individual must let himself be guided by abstract and impersonal signs. He cannot consciously aim at the most gain for others, but only at the most gain for himself and his associates.

This rule of conduct conflicts with the moral instincts we have inherited from the face-to-face society in which the human race for centuries lived hundreds of times longer than in the exchange society of the last 200 years. These moral instincts derive from the small hunting group of 50 or so men, and from the later tribal society in which the concern of each for the known needs of his fellows was essential for the survival of the group.

To these inherited and deeply ingrained emotions, the incentives which make us work for the market give little gratification. The restraints the legal order places on them —such as the respect for another's property, the keeping of promises, and the responsibility for torts—often appear meaningless. So long as independent artisans, craftsmen, tradesmen or merchants numerically predominated in society and shaped opinion, their daily acquaintance with the market taught them its rules, and the commercial standards it had developed were widely accepted. But among employees of large organisations, who have little acquaintance with the market and to whom the rôle of prices as essential signals is largely incomprehensible, the ancestral emotions of morality and justice have re-emerged. The clamour today is for *visible* 'justice'—an allocation of rewards for recognisable merits and 'needs'.

[43]

*Contrived 'social justice' is meaningless; justice develops*
*spontaneously if it generates behaviour that benefits all*

This desire is not only irreconcilable with the signalling and guide functions of prices and, in consequence, destructive of the market. It also raises moral problems to which traditional moral principles provide no answers. The formula which is widely believed to provide an answer, namely, 'social justice', proves when tested to be wholly devoid of content. Beneficial conceptions of justice will develop naturally and persist in a society when they secure conduct which benefits the members of the group which practises them, not when attempts to make them prevail are imposed by force.

*Pursuit of private gain guided by abstract rules of honest conduct does*
*more good for others*

The rules of just individual conduct which the law enforces, and which essentially require honesty, have gained wide acceptance in the Western world because they impartially improved the chances of all individuals to obtain a larger command over the worldly goods for which they strive. But most people find it difficult to understand that the pursuit of gain guided solely by abstract rules of honest conduct may do more good for others we do not know than a conscious, deliberate attempt to do good to them. Yet we in the Western world would certainly never have achieved our present standard of living if individuals had allowed moral feelings about good intentions to prevail, and had consequently forced people to aim at satisfying the needs of individuals they knew directly.

*Return to a less impersonal society would be a return to poverty*

We ought, perhaps, to understand that many well-intentioned, 'compassionate' people dislike this impersonal, abstract society into which they are born and which provides insufficient gratification for their altruistic emotions. But a return to the primitive forms of society for which they yearn, in which doing good can be expressed directly in everyday life, would also mean a return to the extreme poverty which has been abolished in the Western world. The poverty, moreover, would be much more severe if the present millions of population had to be fed by a process of deliberate direction of the use of resources to satisfy the wants of people known personally to all producers by hand or brain.

[44]

### Competition: a 'game' of discovery that creates wealth by skill and chance

The competitive search for adaptation to an uncertain future induces us to try to use as fully as possible the dispersed knowledge of continually changing detailed information. This process necessarily becomes a sort of game in which individual success usually depends on a combination of skill and luck which can never be clearly distinguished. The right thing for the individual to do at a given moment—what is both in his own and in the general interest—must depend on the accidental position into which history has placed him. We have learned to play this game of *discovery*, which we call 'competition', because the communities that experimented with it and gradually improved its rules have flourished above others. Consequently they have been imitated. But the outcome of the game, the rules of which require people to take the fullest advantage of the opportunities that come their way to serve both themselves and others, can be no more 'just' than that of any game of chance.

All we can ask is that the players behave honestly and do not cheat, and that the rules are the same for all. But we cannot make even the starting positions the same if the game is to serve its purpose of inducing people to make the best of their peculiar knowledge of circumstances and their peculiar skills. If the abstract signals of prices are to give correct guidance, the value which the services required have for consumers must be offered to *all* potential suppliers alike, irrespective of their 'needs' or merits. Those whose position and knowledge enable them to make the most gain must be tempted into the game, in order that their competition brings down prices for everyone else. If the individual is to be free to decide what to produce, he must be paid, whether the result of his efforts is due to skill or luck. To try to make this remuneration correspond to what is imagined to be 'socially just' would thus, in practice, be anti-social and destructive of the national wealth.

### High-minded men intent on doing visible good would destroy wealth

An economist necessarily becomes a student of conflicts of values. He must constantly draw attention to the existence of such conflicts which people, in their dreams of good works, tend to ignore. He must warn them not to under-estimate the importance of those values of protection against destitution and starvation which are now largely assured and taken for granted, and not to sacrifice them to the lure of new ones—selfless compassion or 'caring'—which are not yet realised.

What the economist is thus sometimes obliged to tell people is that to follow the advice of what are commonly regarded as 'good men', because their views appeal to deeply ingrained moral emotions, may destroy the whole framework within which those new ambitions of doing good seem to be achievable. Unfortunately, the real goodness of a moral view does not depend on the high-mindedness of its exponents. The good done in everyday life would be undermined by acting on high-minded advice because it would destroy the peaceful co-operation of free men using their own knowledge for their own purposes.

Moral rules prove themselves in time by demonstrating that they conduce to the general welfare of all members of society as a whole, not by benefiting particular high-minded groups that wish to impose their notion of what is moral upon society. In other words, what is good for society does not necessarily correspond with the advice proffered by those individuals who are regarded as good, even if they are revered as near-saintly. It is determined by the welfare of the community which practises the moral rules. A set of moral beliefs supported by the moral leaders of a society, theological or secular, may become a grave obstacle to the achievement of such necessary requirements of a coherent society as peace and good prospects for individuals to attain the goals for which they strive and which conduce to the benefit of all.

### The interaction of morals and institutions

In a society of free men, such non-viable morals are likely to disappear with the decline of the community which practises them. It is different once they become embedded in its institutions. A vague idea like that of 'social justice' will lead to the creation of an apparatus charged with putting right by force what is thought to be wrong. Such institutions, expected to apply a moral code that does not exist, come under irresistible pressure from many sectional interests to remedy their respective social grievances. This pressure forces the institutions to invent new rules which satisfy the sectional demands, but which increasingly obstruct the functioning of the self-ordering market mechanism. In this process, unclear moral ideas lead to the creation of national (and now, increasingly, even international) institutions which are then under a political necessity to design new rules that may have very little to do with the initial moral aims which led to their creation. I sometimes wonder whether this interaction, in which moral beliefs create institutions which, in turn, produce moral conceptions very different from those which gave rise to the institutions, is not the true story of the rise and fall of civilisations.

Examples of such national and international institutions are minimum wages depriving juveniles and immigrants of chances of jobs, or support by the International Labour Office depriving under-developed countries of the possibility of competition.

*Recovery of Britain requires rejection of 'high-minded' politicians; political determination of income has wasted resources and destroyed wealth*

This conclusion raises a further question: Can a people which finds it has developed destructive morals save itself? If those precepts have remained 'moral' in the *true* sense of the word— that they are not enforced by organised power—then no doubt self-salvation is still possible. But it will require the decline of the influence of the groups which led opinion, and their place will have to be taken by others who are prepared to disregard such *harmful* principles. The struggle for the recovery of Britain may thus mean a struggle against those long regarded as the 'good' people, whose 'social conscience' led them to try to impose some ideal design on the distribution of incomes. These are the politicians in all parties, in the trade unions, supported by well-meaning but muddled people in high places.

There is, of course, no reason why, in a community with the degree of wealth generally achieved by Western nations, we should not be able to provide *outside* the market a uniform minimum income for all adults who, for one reason or another, cannot earn more in the market. But, in view of the extent to which in Britain today relative wages and prices are determined politically, it must be wondered how the country can still produce anything at all at prices which have to be internationally competitive. And it is impossible not to be pessimistic about the future of Britain until the basic source of the inability to earn more from international trade is removed.

The threat that the weakness may be made even worse by further resort to central direction and planning, advocated by some politicians, raises not only economic but also political spectres.

### *Keynes wrong again: aiming for heaven makes life hell*

Some people still place trust in the belief that the sound basic instincts of the British people will protect the nation from such a course. But this confidence is justified only so long as individuals are free to select or reject moral ideas according to whether they enhance or damage the health of the community.

It is different when ideals are forced upon them by the coercive powers of government. National character certainly shapes institutions, but, in the long run, institutions also shape national character. It is, therefore, a dangerous delusion to believe, as Lord Keynes wrote to me at the end of his comments on my 1944 book, *The Road to Serfdom*, that

> 'dangerous acts can be done safely in a community which thinks and feels rightly which would be the way to hell if they were executed by those who think and feel wrongly'.

I fear that the German poet Friedrich Hölderlin saw more clearly when, almost 150 years earlier, he wrote:

> 'What has always made the state a hell on earth has been precisely that man has tried to make it his heaven.'

# PART IV

# The Trade Unions and Britain's Economic Decline

So far I have discussed the general principles of a market economy. I now turn to what is widely recognised as the crucial debility in Britain's economic future but which is usually regarded as politically insoluble.

Trade unions, in their present form, have become part of the British way of life, and their power has become politically sacrosanct. But economic decline has also become part of the British way of life, and few people are willing to accept that as sacrosanct. Many British people are beginning to see the connection between the two. Yet this insight is in such conflict with what most of them believe the trade unions have achieved for the mass of wage-earners that they cannot see a remedy. This dilemma overlooks the unique privileges the unions enjoy in Britain, which have placed them in a position where they are forced to be anti-social, as even one of their friends, Baroness Wootton, has had to admit.

### False claims to benefit the population as a whole

Unions have gained the public support they still enjoy by their pretence of benefiting the working population at large. They probably did achieve this aim in their early years when more or less immobile workers sometimes faced a single factory-owner. I do not, of course, deny the trade unions their historical merits or question their right to exist as voluntary organisations. Indeed, I believe that everybody, unless he has voluntarily renounced it, ought to have the right to join a trade union. But neither ought anyone to have the right to force others to do so. I am even prepared to agree that *everybody* ought to have the *right* to strike, so far as he does not thereby break a contract or the law has not conferred a monopoly on the enterprise in which he is engaged. But I am convinced that nobody ought to have the right to *force* others to strike.

### Trade unions' legal privileges obstruct working-class prosperity

Such would be the position if the general principles of law applicable to all other citizens applied also to the trade unions and their members. But in 1906, in a typical act of buying the

[51]

swing-vote of a minority, the then Liberal Government passed the Trade Disputes Act which, as A. V. Dicey justly put it (*in Law and Public Opinion in England* (1914)), conferred

'upon a trade union a freedom from civil liability for the commission of even the most heinous wrong by the union or its servant, and in short confer[red] upon every trade union a privilege and protection not possessed by any other person or body of persons, whether corporate or incorporate. ... [it] makes the trade union a privileged body exempted from the ordinary law of the land. No such privileged body has ever before been created by an English Parliament [and] it stimulates among workmen the fatal illusion that [they] should aim at the attainment not of equality, but of privilege.'

These legalised powers of the unions have become the biggest obstacle to raising the living standards of the working class as a whole. They are the chief cause of the unnecessarily big differences between the best- and worst-paid workers. They are the prime source of unemployment. They are the main reason for the decline of the British economy in general.

### *Trade union members gain by exploiting other workers*

The crucial truth, which is not generally understood, is that all the powers employed by individual trade unions to raise the remuneration of their members rest on depriving other workers of opportunities. This truth was apparently understood, in the past, by the more reasonable trade union leaders. Twenty-three years ago, the then chairman of the Trades Union Congress could still say that he did

'not believe that the trade union movement of Great Britain can live for much longer on the basis of compulsion. Must people belong to us or starve, whether they like our policies or not? No. I believe the trade union card is an honour to be conferred, not a badge which signifies that you have got to do something whether you like it or not. We want the right to exclude people from our union if necessary, and we cannot do this on the basis of "Belong or Starve" '.

Thus Mr Charles (now Lord) Geddes.

There has evidently been a complete change. The present ability of any trade union to obtain better terms for its members rests chiefly on its legalised power to *prevent other workers from earning as good an income as they otherwise might*. It is thus maintained, literally, by the exploitation of those not permitted to

[52]

do work that they would like to do. The élite of the British working class may still profit as a result, although even this has now become doubtful. But they certainly derive their relative advantage by keeping workers who are *worse* off from improving their position. These groups acquire their advantage at the expense of those they prevent from bettering themselves by doing work in which they could earn more—though somewhat less than those who claim a monopoly.

### Free society threatened by union curtailment of access to jobs

If a free society is to continue, no monopoly can be allowed to use physical force to maintain its privileged position and to threaten to deprive the public of essential services that other workers are able and willing to render. Yet all the most harmful practices of British trade unions derive from their being allowed forcefully to prevent outsiders from offering their services to the public on their own terms. The chief instances of such legal powers are intimidatory picketing, preventing non-members from doing particular kinds of jobs such as 'demarcation' rules, and the closed shop. Yet all these restrictive practices are prohibited in most of the more prosperous Western countries.

### Union restrictive practices have hurt the working man

It is more than doubtful, however, whether in the long run these selfish practices have improved the real wages of even those workers whose unions have been most successful in driving up their relative wages—compared with what they would have been in the absence of trade unions. It is certain, and could not be otherwise, that the average level of attainable real wages of British workers as a whole has thereby been substantially lowered. Such practices have substantially reduced the productivity potential of British labour generally. They have turned Britain, which at one time had the highest wages in Europe, into a relatively low-wage economy.

### British price structure paralysed by political wage determination

A large economy can be prosperous only if it relies on competitive prices to co-ordinate individual effort by condensing all the information fed into the market by many thousands of individuals. The effect of the present system of wage determination in Britain is that the country no longer has an internal price structure to guide the economic use of resources. This is almost entirely due to the rigidity of politically determined wages. If it is no longer possible to know the most efficient use of the natural talents of the British people, it is because relative wages no longer reflect the relative scarcity of skills. Even their relative scarcity is no longer determined by objective facts about the real conditions of supply and demand, but by an artificial product of the arbitrary decisions of legally tolerated monopolies.

## Impersonal nature of market decisions makes them acceptable

Prices or wages cannot be a matter of 'justice' if the economic system is to function. Whether it is necessary for maintaining or increasing the national income to draw people into tool-making or services, or to discourage entry into entertainment or sociological research, has nothing to do with the 'justice' or the merits or the 'needs' of those affected. In the real world, nobody can know where people are required but the market, which absorbs and digests the myriad bits of information possessed by all who buy or sell in it. And it is precisely because the decision is not the opinion of an identifiable person (like a Minister or Commissar) or a group of men (like a Cabinet or Politbureau) but results from impersonal signals in a process that no individual or group can control, that makes it tolerable. It would be unbearable if it were the decision of some authority which assigned everyone to his job and determined his reward.

## British governments have supported union coercion

I would be prepared to predict that the average worker's income would rise fastest in a country where relative wages are flexible, and where the exploitation of workers by monopolistic trade union organisations of specialised groups of workers are effectively outlawed. Such exploitation is, however, the chief source of power of individual labour unions in Britain. The result of thus freeing the labour market would inevitably be a structure of relative wages very different from the traditional one now preserved by union power. This result will have to come about if the British economy is to stop decaying.

While a functioning market and trade unions with coercive powers cannot co-exist, yet it is only in the free system of the market that the unions can survive. Yet the unions are destroying the free market through their legalised use of coercion. The widespread use of force to gain at the expense of others has not only been tolerated but also supported by British governments, on the false pretence that it enhances justice and benefits the most needy. Not only is the opposite true; the effect of this tolerance and support of union coercion is to reduce everybody's potential income—except that of trade union officials.

### *Trade unions' legal privileges the chief cause of unemployment*

Impeding increases in productivity and hence real wage growth is not the worst effect of current trade union practices. Even more serious is the extent to which they have become the chief cause of unemployment, for which the market economy is then blamed.

The volume of employment is not a function of the *general* wage level but of the structure of *relative* wages. The contrary belief, still widely held in Britain by economists and politicians, is due to a unique experience of this country. It arose after Britain returned to the gold standard in 1925 at the pre-war parity between sterling and gold, when wages, which had risen considerably during the wartime inflation, proved generally too high for the country to maintain its exports. It was in that very special atmosphere that discussion about the relationship between wages and unemployment started, and the belief came to be held that the crucial factor was the general level of wages. The writings of Keynes unfortunately seemed to support this error.

The situation after 1925 was entirely exceptional. The normal cause of recurrent waves of widespread unemployment is rather a discrepancy between the way in which demand is distributed between products and services, and the proportions in which resources are devoted to producing them. Unemployment is the result of divergent changes in the direction of demand and the techniques of production. If labour is not deployed according to demand for products, there is unemployment. But the most common cause is that, because of excessive credit expansion, over-investment has been encouraged and too many resources have been drawn into the production of capital goods, where they can be employed only so long as the expansion continues or even accelerates. And credit is expanded to appease trade unions that fear their members will lose their jobs, even though it is they themselves who forced wages too high to enable the workers to find jobs at these excessive rates of pay.

### Full employment requires continual changes in relative wages

Once such a misdirection of resources has taken place, tolerably full employment can be restored only by redirecting some of them to other uses. This is, of necessity, a slow process, even when wages are flexible. And so long as substantial unemployment prevails in such a large sector of the economy, it is likely to set up a cumulative process of deflation. Even maintaining total final demand cannot provide a cure, because it will not create employment in the over-expanded capital industries. The unemployment there will continue to operate as a persistent drain on the income stream. It cannot be stopped, or lastingly compensated for, by the expenditure of new paper money printed for the purpose or created in other ways. The attempt to cure it by adding to the supply of money must lead to accelerating inflation. Yet this has been the futile policy of recent British governments.

Such unemployment can be effectively cured only by redirecting workers to jobs where they can be lastingly employed. In a free society, this redirection requires a change in relative wages to make prospects less attractive in occupations or industries where labour is in surplus and more attractive where the demand for labour is expanding. This is *the essential mechanism which alone can correct a misdirection of labour* once it has occurred in a society where workers are free to choose their jobs.

Short of very special circumstances such as those after 1925, there is no reason why it should ever be necessary for the general level of wages to fall. But it is not possible to keep a market economy working *at full speed*, which is what the workers would like, without *some* wages occasionally falling while others rise. Full employment cannot be maintained by preserving a conventional, outdated wage structure, but only by adjusting wages in each sector to changing demands—raising some wages by lowering others.

[56]

## Keynes's responsibility for 'the final disaster'

The final disaster we owe mainly to Lord Keynes. His erroneous conception that employment could be directly controlled by regulating aggregate demand through monetary policy shifted responsibility for employment from the trade unions to government. This error relieved trade unions of the responsibility to adjust their wage demands so as to sell as much work as possible, and misrepresented full employment entirely as a function of government monetary policy. For 40 years it has thus made the price mechanism ineffective in the labour market by preventing wages from acting as a signal to workers and employers. As a result there is divided responsibility: the trade unions are allowed to enforce their wage demands without regard to the effect on employment, and government is expected to create the demand at which the available supply of work can be sold at the prevailing (or even higher) wages. Inevitably the consequence is continuous and accelerating inflation.

## Futility of negotiating reform with union leaders until deprived of legal privileges

It is an illusion to imagine that the problems Britain now faces can be solved by negotiation with the present trade union leaders. They owe their power precisely to the scope for abusing the privileges which the law has granted them. It is the rank and file of the workers, including many trade union members, who ultimately suffer from this abuse. I believe they could be helped to understand this cause of their suffering. Their support must be obtained if the system that is destroying Britain's wealth and well-being is to be changed.

One of the more recent general secretaries of the Trades Union Congress, the late George Woodcock, wrote about 'the fear and dislike in which many of our own people seem to hold our own trade unions'. A political party in which trade unions have a major constitutional rôle cannot strike at the source of their power. If I were responsible for the policy of the Conservative Party, I would rather be defeated at the polls than be charged with policy but without a clear mandate to remove the legal sources of excessive trade union power. This a trade union party, of course, can never do. The only hope is that an appeal to a large number of workers over the

[57]

heads of their present leaders will lead to the demand for a reduction in their powers.

### No salvation for Britain until union privileges are revoked

There can be no salvation for Britain until the special privileges granted to the trade unions three-quarters of a century ago are revoked. Average real wages of British workers would undoubtedly be higher, and their chances of finding employment better, if the wages paid in different occupations were again determined by the market and if all limitations on the work an individual is allowed to do were removed.

Britain can improve her position in the world market, and hence the price in work effort at which her population can be fed, only by allowing the market to bring about a restructuring of her whole internal price system. What is ossified in Britain is not the skill of her entrepreneurs or workers, but the price structure and the indispensable discipline it imposes. The present British economic system no longer signals what has to be done and no longer rewards those who do it or penalises those who fail to do it.

# PART V

# Reform of Trade Union Privilege the Price of Salvation in the 1980s*

*An edited version of an article, 'The powerful reasons for curbing union powers', published in *The Times*, 10 October 1978.

Sometimes one is forced to doubt whether it is still doctrinaire blindness rather than sinister intention that leads politicians in Britain and elsewhere to invert the truth. One of the most glaring examples has been the attempt to represent the present British trade unions as free institutions. They were when they fought for freedom of association and thereby gained the support of all believers in liberty. They unfortunately retained the support of some naïve pseudo-liberals after they had become the only privileged institution licensed to use coercion without law.

The coercion on which their present power rests is the coercion of other workers who are deterred by the threat of violence from offering their labour on their own terms. The coercion of enterprise is always secondary, and operates through depriving other workers of their opportunities.

### 'Open enemies'

The unions have of course now become the open enemies of the ideal of freedom of association by which they once gained the sympathy of the true liberals. Freedom of association means the freedom to decide whether one wants to join an association or not. Such freedom no longer exists for most workers. The present unions offer to a skilled worker only the choice between joining and starving, and it is solely by keeping non-members out of jobs that they can raise the wages of particular groups of workers above the level they would reach in a free market.

There are certainly many useful tasks unions can perform with respect to the internal organisations of enterprises—questions on which the arrangements of large organisations depend. But they cease to operate beneficially when they are conceded the power of keeping non-members out of a job, or refuse to work with others who prefer different contracts from those which they obtain for their members. The higher wages the unions can thus obtain for those who can be employed at their terms are gained at the expense of those who cannot be thus employed.

Like all other monopolistic control of prices its main effect is to suspend the process which brings about the balancing of demand and supply in the different sectors of economic activity. It is in this way that the licensed use of force by the trade unions to determine a structure of relative wages which the individual unions or smaller groups of workers regard as attainable has become the chief obstacle to a high and stable level of employment.

It is a complete inversion of the truth to represent the unions as improving the prospect of employment at high wages. They have become in Britain the chief cause of unemployment and the falling standard of living of the working class.

I prefer to believe it is doctrinaire blindness rather than a devious attempt to destroy the existing order which can make a politician deny this obvious truth. For a country depending for its livelihood on international trade the endeavour to shelter relative wages against the forces of the international market can have no other effect than growing unemployment at falling real wages. Britain has been led into a position in which it has become impossible to know how its labour force can be deployed most productively.

### The Foot confusion

It was the most extraordinary part of Michael Foot's outburst a year or two ago that he represented unions as simultaneously a part of free institutions and the restriction of their coercive powers as a cause of unemployment. The reason why I believe that the licence to use coercion conceded to unions some 70 years ago should be withdrawn is precisely that their actions have become the chief cause of unemployment. They bring this about in two ways. The first is the obvious one of an increased demand for some product being absorbed by an increase of the wages of the workers already employed in it rather than by an influx of additional workers, leaving out in the cold those in the industries from which demand has turned.

The second way is less understood but even more serious because it is more permanent. At wages higher than those which would prevail in a free market, employers must, in order to be able to pay them, use the limited amount of capital that is available in a manner which will require fewer workers for a given output. It is true that higher wages can enforce 'rationalisation': they bring this about by making it necessary to use the available capital for equipping a smaller number of workers with more capital per head, leaving correspondingly less for the rest.

## J. M. Keynes's palliative

All this had been well understood long ago. It was initially only J. M. Keynes's despair about the political impossibility of making wages again flexible which led him to resort to the palliative of temporarily reducing real wages by inflation. But one may thus for a time evade the difficulties caused by a rigid wage *level*, but not those caused by an artificially fixed structure of *relative* wages. This is what apparently even some of the more experienced trade union leaders are beginning to understand, but what the illusionists and demagogues of the Labour Party refuse to recognise.

In an ever-changing world there is as little chance of the market for labour ever being cleared with rigid relative wages based on some traditional standards as there would be for the different commodities at rigid relative prices. And the power to stop the whole supply of an essential element of production is, of course, the power to kill enterprise. There will usually exist some reserves which can sustain life for a time even after an enterprise has been mortally wounded. However, I fear in many instances the process of capital shrinkage is merely temporarily concealed by inflation but will manifest itself as soon as inflation stops, as it must sooner or later.

It will then be vain to ask government to preserve the existing jobs. The Government can do nothing to force the world to buy British goods. Indeed, the pressure on it to secure particular jobs is the most certain means progressively to reduce the productivity of British workers and their earning power in international exchange.

## Fools' paradise

Britain can scarcely hope to be self-sufficient even with general prosperity; but she can certainly not be a wealthy country without constant redirection of efforts which in recent times have been so lamentably impeded by the political necessity of enabling people to carry on as before by providing the means out of the pockets of others. The longer we allow the number to grow in their present employment while producing what the world market will not buy at prices adequate to maintain them at their present level, the greater will be the ultimate catastrophe when the fools' paradise collapses.

[63]

There is no hope of Great Britain maintaining her position in international trade—and for her people that means no hope of maintaining their already reduced standard of living—unless the unions are deprived of their coercive powers. So long as they possess them, even the wisest union leaders can, as we see every day, be forced by little groups to exercise them. This is killing enterprise after enterprise and causing a continuous dissipation of capital, the full effect of which we have not yet experienced. As a result of a mistake of legislation in the past they have Britain by the throat and cannot understand they are killing the goose which lays the golden eggs.

I am not qualified to judge what is today politically possible. That depends on prevailing opinion. All I can say with conviction is that, *so long as general opinion makes it politically impossible to deprive the trade unions of their coercive powers, an economic recovery of Great Britain is also impossible.*

It is sufficiently alarming when one watches developments in Britain from the inside. But one is reduced to complete despair when one observes what is happening in the rest of the world while Britain remains paralysed by the consequences of the privileges irresponsibly conceded to the trade unions by law. When one watches how even Japan is now being beaten in ever more fields by South Korea and other newcomers who have discovered the benefits of free markets, one cannot but shudder when one asks how in a few years' time Britain is to get the food to feed her people.

### Will Britain pay the price of the union 'sacred cow'?

This is not merely a question of whether Britain can do without Japanese or Korean cars or other products. It is a question of how other people can be made to buy British ships, or shoes, or steel, or textiles, or chemicals, when not only Japanese and Korean factories and shipyards produce them more efficiently and cheaply, but more and more other people surpass Britain in an astounding versatility—and when not only British scientists and engineers but increasingly also skilled British workers find that they can do better in countries whose business structure has not been ossified by trade union restrictions.

A drastic change may still provide an outlet, but after another decade during which nobody dares to touch the sacred cow, it will certainly be too late.

[64]

# FROM TAFF VALE
# TO TEBBIT

*A Postscript on British Trade Unions
and the Law*

CHARLES G. HANSON
*Lecturer in Economics,
University of Newcastle upon Tyne*

# THE AUTHOR

CHARLES G. HANSON, MA (Cantab.), PHD (Newcastle upon Tyne), Lecturer in Economics at the University of Newcastle upon Tyne since 1962, Special Adviser to the House of Commons Employment Committee, 1980-81, Member of the Council of the Freedom Association since 1982, Labour Relations Adviser to the Institute of Directors since 1983. Editor and co-author of *The Closed Shop* (Gower, 1982) and author and co-author of numerous articles on labour relations in journals since 1965, including the *Journal of Management Studies*, *The Economic History Review*, and bank reviews. Co-author of the *Employment Policy* Report of the Adam Smith Institute (1983), part of the Omega Project, and an adjunct scholar of the Adam Smith Institute since 1983. Contributor to the publications of the Institute of Economic Affairs, including *Trade Unions: A Century of Privilege?* (Occasional Paper 38, 1973), papers in *The Long Debate on Poverty* (IEA Readings No. 9, 1972, 2nd Edn. 1974) and *Trade Unions: Public Goods or Public 'Bads'?* (IEA Readings No. 17, 1978), and (the *Journal of*) *Economic Affairs*.

'There can be no salvation for Britain until the special privileges granted to the trade unions three-quarters of a century ago are revoked.' (p. 58)

'All I can say with conviction is that, *so long as general opinion makes it politically impossible to deprive the trade unions of their coercive powers, an economic recovery of Great Britain is also impossible.*' (p. 64)

These two breathtaking statements contain the essence of Professor F. A. Hayek's *Hobart Paper*. If they are true, it is impossible to exaggerate their significance. Professor Hayek is insisting that the basic remedy for the 'British disease' is the abolition of the legal privileges which Parliament conferred on the trade unions in the Trade Disputes Act of 1906. This proposal was made in the First Edition of his *Paper*, published in 1980; the events of the last four years have certainly vindicated Professor Hayek's analysis. But much other water, in the shape of labour law reform, has also flowed under the bridge in that period. The re-publication of the *Paper* calls for an examination of some key issues.

The purpose of this Postscript is to answer three questions:

(i) What were the privileges conferred on the unions in 1906 and why have they been significant?

(ii) What privileges remain in 1984 after the reforms of the Employment Acts of 1980 and 1982 and the Trade Union Bill of 1984?

(iii) What step should the Government take next, so that Professor Hayek's proposal may ultimately be carried fully into effect?

## 1. THE PRIVILEGES OF THE TRADE DISPUTES ACT OF 1906 AND THEIR SIGNIFICANCE

The Trade Disputes Act, which followed the General Election of January 1906, was Parliament's answer to the judgement of the House of Lords in the Taff Vale Case, 1901. It was decided there that trade unions were corporately liable for the acts of their agents. Consequently, the Amalgamated Society of Railway Servants, which had been involved in a strike against the Taff Vale Railway Company, was compelled to pay a total of £42,000 (an enormous sum in those days) in damages and costs.

The fundamental question raised by the Taff Vale case was the effect of the Trade Union Act of 1871 and the Conspiracy and Protection of Property Act of 1875. Lord Macnaghten put the question thus in the House of Lords judgement:

'Has the legislature authorised the creation of numerous bodies of men, capable of owning great wealth and of acting by agents, with absolutely no responsibility for the wrong they may do to other persons by the use of that wealth and the employment of those agents? In my opinion Parliament has done nothing of the kind. I can find nothing in the Acts of 1871 and 1875 ... from beginning to end, to warrant such a notion.'[1]

This totally reasonable answer caused uproar among the unions at the time when the Labour Party had so recently been born and was quickly becoming a lusty child. Something had to be done, and the immediate response was the establishment of a Royal Commission which included Sidney Webb, a trade union sympathiser and considered an expert in trade union law. The majority report of the Commission, which Sidney Webb signed, recommended some protection for trade union activity but argued that the Taff Vale judgement was sound law. It said:

'The objections against disturbing the law as laid down in the Taff Vale case appear insurmountable. There is no rule of law so elementary, so universal or so indispensable as the rule that a wrong-doer should be made to redress his wrong. If Trade Unions were exempt from this liability they would be the only exception, and it would then be right that the exception should be removed.'[2]

[1] Quoted in H. A. Clegg, A. Fox and A. F. Thompson, *A History of British Trade Unions since 1889*, Vol. 1: 1889-1910, Oxford University Press, 1964, p. 315.

[2] *Report of the Royal Commission on Trade Disputes and Trade Combinations*, Cd. 2825, HMSO, 1906, p. 2.

The Liberal Government of 1906 accepted this argument. But politicians who had been anxious for trade union support at the polls forced the Government to legislate contrary to its better judgement. As the Webbs put it in describing the scene in the House of Commons:

'Member after member rose from different parts of the House to explain that they had pledged themselves to vote for the complete immunity which Trade Unions were supposed to have been granted in 1871. Nothing less than this would suffice; and the most powerful Government hitherto known was constrained, in spite of the protests of lawyers and employers, to pass into law the Trade Disputes Act of 1906.'[1]

How exactly did this Act provide 'the complete immunity which trade unions were supposed to have been granted in 1871'? That is not at all well understood.

### Trade union privileges

#### (i) Corporate immunity

Trade union immunities, or privileges, are of two main kinds. First, Parliament has provided immunity for trade unions as corporate bodies. Secondly, immunity has been provided for trade union officials. These immunities were laid down in Sections 4(1) and 3 respectively of the 1906 Act. Section 4(1) read as follows:

'An action against a trade union, whether of workmen or masters, or against any members or officials thereof on behalf of themselves and all other members of the trade union in respect of any tortious act[2] alleged to have been committed by or on behalf of the trade union, shall not be entertained by any court.'

This section put trade unions above the law. In future they could do what they liked and cause the most immense damages without being subject to any legal sanctions whatsoever. It was of this section that the great constitutional lawyer A. V. Dicey wrote in 1914 that:

'It makes a trade union a privileged body exempted from the

---

[1] S. and B. Webb, *The History of Trade Unionism*, 1920 Edition, published by the Webbs themselves 'for the Trade Unionists of the United Kingdom', p. 606.

[2] A tortious act, or tort, is any wrong, not arising out of contract, for which there is a remedy by compensation or damages. Torts include libel, negligence and strike activity.

ordinary law of the land. No such privileged body has ever before been deliberately created by an English Parliament.'[1]

And the Webbs added their condemnation; they said the clause conferred upon the unions:

> 'an extraordinary and unlimited immunity, however great may be the damage caused, and however unwarranted the act, which most lawyers, as well as all employers, regard as nothing less than monstrous.'[2]

In a prophetic footnote to this protest, the Webbs suggested that 'Trade Unionists would be well advised not to presume too far on this apparently absolute immunity from legal proceedings'. But given the determination of Parliament to maintain the privilege for 65 years until the Heath Government's attempted reform, it is, perhaps, not surprising that this piece of advice was ignored.

### (ii) *Immunity of trade union officials*

The immunities which Section 3 of the 1906 Act gave to *persons* acting 'in contemplation or furtherance of a trade dispute' were complementary to the *corporate* immunities but slightly less sweeping. They raised the fundamental question of how a 'trade dispute' would be defined in the courts. Would it be lawful for trade union officials to spread a strike way beyond the boundaries of the original dispute? That question was to come to the fore in the 1970s.

The importance of these extraordinary privileges was (and still is) clearly enormous. Two aspects in particular are worthy of special attention—the economic aspects and the political/constitutional aspects.

Adam Smith had laid down the principle in 1776 that 'Consumption is the sole end and purpose of all production',[3] and he had gone on to say that:

> 'the interest of the producer ought to be attended to, only so far as it may be necessary for promoting that of the consumer. The maxim is so perfectly self-evident, that it would be absurd to attempt to prove it. But in the mercantile system, the interest of

[1] A. V. Dicey, *Law and Public Opinion in England* (1914), Macmillan, 2nd Edition, 1963, p. xlvi.

[2] S. and B. Webb, *op. cit*, p. 606.

[3] A. Smith, *The Wealth of Nations*, Cannan Edition, Methuen, 1904, Vol. II, p. 179.

the consumer is almost constantly sacrificed to that of the producer; and it seems to consider production, and not consumption,
as the ultimate end and object of all industry and commerce.'[1]

By the second half of the 19th century, the Smithian philosophy
had prevailed. Mercantilism was dead and Britain had become
the 'workshop of the world' and the greatest trading nation
the world had ever known. But competition and free trade are
uncomfortable. Continuous change and adaptation become
necessary in response to changing demands and tastes. There
is a temptation to withdraw from the fray and to pretend that
the world is a quiet, stable place. The Trade Disputes Act was
the clearest possible sign that the British people had succumbed
to this temptation and had decided to turn their backs on
the economic philosophy which had stood them in good stead
during the 19th century. To give producer groups the kind
of privileges enshrined in the 1906 Act was to ensure that, in
Britain, consumption would eventually be subordinated to
production. Sooner or later, freedom of consumer choice would
be replaced by producer dictation.

### Above the law, equal with Parliament

But the political and constitutional aspect of the 1906 Act was
no less significant than its economic aspect. When Parliament
put trade unions above the law, it put them on a par with
itself. In other words, Parliament invited the unions to play
a major part in the legislative process, and even in one of the
most crucial areas of that process—levying taxes to pay for
public services. For to put trade unions above the law is to
allow them, within limits, to decide their members' wages in
'essential' monopoly services. And during the 20th century
Parliament has shown immense enthusiasm for establishing
state monopoly in the supply of 'essential' services, of which
water, gas and electricity are three of the most obvious
examples. The establishment of these monopolies alongside
the provisions of the 1906 Act in effect gave the workers in
them the power to set their own wages. Part of the cost of this
labour may be regarded as its true market price. The other
part, although paid by consumers through their water rate or
electricity or gas bills, is really a tax which Parliament has
authorised those trade unionists to impose. If the tax element

[1] *Ibid.*

[71]

in the charge is less than it might be, this is simply a reflection of the unions' reluctance to exert their monopoly bargaining power to the full. That bargaining power has been given to them by Parliament and the members are, therefore, fully justified in following the example of the waterworkers in 1983 and using it as and when they wish.

For most of the 20th century, Parliament has created a strange anomaly in essential services. It has placed an obligation on monopoly suppliers to maintain an efficient and economic service but has given their trade unions an unlimited right to strike! Clearly this is a highly unstable situation: the producer interest will more and more take precedence over consumers; and the government itself will, from time to time, be forced to surrender to groups of well-organised workers.

As this situation became increasingly obvious in the 1960s and 1970s, public opinion began to question the unlimited right to strike. In 1970, a Conservative Government led by Mr Edward Heath was elected to office pledged to reform and modify the law. This pledge was kept in the Industrial Relations Act of 1971, an unduly legalistic measure which repealed most of the earlier legislation, including the 1906 Act, and made the modified immunities conditional upon registration by the unions. Thus the unions were able to undermine the Act by refusing to register, and, following its failure and a General Election, the new Labour Government, at the behest of the unions, re-introduced the 1906 privileges between 1974 and 1979 and extended them where possible. By 1979, trade unions and their officials not only had the legal right to force employees to join a union under threat of dismissal without compensation where employers had agreed to a closed shop.[1] They also had the right to spread a strike to parties quite unconnected with the original dispute without fear of redress.

In reaction to union excesses in the winter of 1978-79, however, public opinion re-asserted itself. The Conservative Government elected in 1979 was pledged to reduce the immunities, and despite rising unemployment it was re-elected with a much increased majority in 1983. What has the Thatcher Government achieved in the reform of trade union law?

---

[1] This situation led to the British Government being condemned by the European Court at Strasbourg in 1981 in the case of Young, James and Webster *v.* United Kingdom, for infringing basic human rights contrary to Article 11 of the European Convention on Human Rights.

## 2. The Employment Acts of 1980 and 1982 and the Trade Union Bill of 1984

The Employment Act of 1980 modified the law on the closed shop to eliminate the worst excesses of the period 1974 to 1979. It also cut back union immunities in two ways:

(a) secondary picketing was made illegal; and

(b) immunity was removed from trade union officials who organised certain secondary strikes.

### The law on picketing

As for picketing, it must be emphasised that the law has *never* permitted anything more than picketing for the purpose of 'peacefully obtaining or communicating information, or peacefully persuading any person to work or abstain from working'.[1] It is unlikely that picketing by more than a handful of pickets can ever be peaceful as defined by the law. This explains why the 'Code of Practice on Picketing', issued by Parliament in 1980, recommends that the number of pickets should not normally 'exceed six at any entrance to a workplace' and that 'frequently a smaller number will be appropriate' (para. 31 of the Code). The Code of Practice clearly indicates that mass, intimidatory picketing of the kind deliberately organised by certain sections of the National Union of Mineworkers in 1984 and on earlier occasions is in blatant breach of the civil and criminal law. The deafening silence of most senior trade union officials and many senior Labour Party politicians condones this kind of action and encourages the substitution of mob rule for the rule of law.

It will be noted that neither of the reforms of the Employment Act of 1980 affected the immunities of *trade unions themselves* in any way. They were directed at pickets and union officials; the funds of the unions remained fully protected. Many commentators were of the view that nothing could be done about this problem because if the law was changed it could not be enforced.

Mr Norman Tebbit, whom Mrs Thatcher appointed Secretary of State for Employment in 1981 in place of Mr James Prior, disagreed. His Employment Act of 1982 had three main provisions:

[1] *Trade Union and Labour Relations Act, 1974*, Section 15(b).

[73]

(a) Much stricter controls were placed upon the closed shop, and money was made available to compensate workers who had been unreasonably dismissed in the period 1974-80 for not joining a union.

(b) The definition of a 'trade dispute' was narrowed so that the immunity available to union officials acting 'in contemplation or furtherance of a trade dispute' was significantly cut back. The immunity was henceforth available only in 'a dispute between workers and their employer which relates wholly or mainly to' the terms and conditions of employment and closely related issues. Thus politically-motivated strikes no longer enjoy immunity.

The crucial importance of this change became apparent in November 1983 when, in *Mercury Communications Ltd v. Stanley and Another*, the Court of Appeal granted Mercury an injunction against a strike called to prevent the linking of its telecommunications with British Telecom. If the Secretary of State had not changed the definition of a trade dispute in 1982 the politically-motivated strike would have been lawful, and a major part of the Government's privatisation and competition policy might have been frustrated by trade union opposition.

(c) The most radical provision of the 1982 Act was in Section 15, which repealed Section 14 of the Trade Union and Labour Relations Act of 1974. It had the effect of removing the immunity for actions in tort from *trade unions* in four cases 'if, but only if, the act was authorised or endorsed by a responsible person',[1] that is, a trade union official. Trade union action is not now immune from liability:

(i) where it is not taken 'in contemplation or furtherance of a trade dispute' under the new, narrower definition of a trade dispute; or

(ii) where it is taken in the course of unlawful picketing; or

(iii) where it entails unlawful secondary action; or

(iv) where it is taken to impose union membership or recognition requirements on another employer.

[1] *Employment Act 1982*, Section 15(2).

Damages may vary from £10,000 for a small union to £250,000 for a large one, but employers will normally seek an inter-locutory injunction rather than damages. What an employer wants is to be able to carry on his business. If an injunction is granted and the union defies it, it becomes guilty of the serious offence of contempt of court and there is then no limit to the fines which may be imposed.

This aspect of the new law was tested in *Stockport Messenger Group v. National Graphical Association*, where the NGA defied an injunction and continued to picket a newspaper printing works. Eventually, the entire assets (about £10 million) of the NGA were sequestrated (seized by the courts) and the union called off the illegal action and conceded defeat. There is, then, evidence that the new legislation can be effective.

### The 1984 Trade Union Bill: secret ballots

What further measures are included in the Trade Union Bill which is likely to become effective in the Autumn of 1984? As to trade union immunities, the object of this modest measure is simply to persuade the unions to allow their members to express their views in a secret ballot before being called out on strike. Part II (Sections 7 and 8) of the Bill is currently being revised to provide that no immunity shall be available to a union which calls a strike, or other action which involves a breach of the contract of employment, unless a majority of all union members concerned have voted, in a secret ballot, in favour of the action to be taken. The trade unions are in some difficulty in opposing this measure, which is supported by a large majority of trade union members. There is a distinct weariness, even among union members, with the undemocratic, bullying methods of some union officials.

Once the Trade Union Bill has become law and the closed shop provisions of the Employment Act of 1982 have come fully into effect (in November 1984), very considerable inroads will have been made into the grossly excessive trade union im-munities which existed in 1979. It has already become clear that this 'step-by-step' method of labour law reform, which the Thatcher Government wisely embarked upon after the bitter experience of the failure of the 1971 Act, can be very effective. But where does the Government go from here? Should it now call a halt and rest on its laurels?

That would seem to be the intention of Mr Tom King, who took over as Secretary of State for Employment in late 1983 and who has stated publicly that the Government would not be rushed into further legislation on trade unions. Such a lethargic approach is, of course, quite unacceptable to those who agree with Professor Hayek that the removal of trade union privilege is a pre-condition of economic recovery. The momentum of reform must be maintained. The Government should now be making its plans for the next step so that further legislation can be presented to Parliament in 1985.

### 3. The Next Step in Trade Union Law Reform

The 'step-by-step' approach to labour law reform has proved its effectiveness. But a series of amending Acts has left the law in an almost unintelligible state. Even legal experts now face perplexing problems in disentangling the law on trade union immunities. The next step should be taken in the context of a consolidation and simplification of this law, now contained in the Trade Union and Labour Relations Act of 1974 as amended by the Trade Union and Labour Relations (Amendment) Act of 1976, the Employment Acts of 1980 and 1982, and (by late 1984) the Trade Union Act of 1984.

This absurdly complex situation must be unravelled by a consolidating Act which repeals all of these measures as well as the Trade Union Act of 1913 and the Trade Unions (Amalgamations, etc.) Act of 1964.

Consolidation on its own is not, however, enough. In their manifesto for the General Election of June 1983, the Conservatives said: 'The nation is entitled to expect that the operation of essential services should not be disrupted', and the electorate provided a more than adequate majority in the House of Commons for the Government to give meaning to those words. The 1984 Trade Union Bill provides that trade union immunities are conditional upon a pre-strike ballot being held. But if workers in 'essential' services vote in favour of a strike, the law will still permit them to strike for as long as they like for as large a pay increase as they can extract from their monopoly employer—the government. In other words, nothing has yet been done to prevent employees in essential services from holding the nation to ransom whenever they wish to do so.

### No-strike contract in essential services

This situation must not be allowed to continue. The only effective remedy is, *first*, for immunities to be removed entirely from unions which organise employees in certain essential services, notably those whose withdrawal immediately threatens the health and safety of the population at large.

*Secondly*, all employees in those services should be required to sign a new contract of employment including a no-strike clause, so that it is clearly understood that the strike weapon is inadmissible as a method of resolving disputes in those essential 'public' or private monopoly services.

*Thirdly*, other 'last-resort' methods of settling disputes would then have to be provided. This has been achieved for the police and the armed forces for many years, so it is clearly not an impossible task. It will become easier as the rate of inflation falls and the Government becomes increasingly determined to operate effective cash limits with stable or falling total public expenditure.

A *fourth* reform should also be undertaken. Currently, all secondary picketing is unlawful. However, some secondary *strikes*, especially those at suppliers or customers of the firm in dispute, are lawful. In other words, the law permits trade unions to cripple or destroy firms whose labour relations are in good order and have no dispute with their own workforce. This anomaly must be ended, and the law on immunities brought into line with the law on picketing by making *all* secondary strikes illegal.

### Towards the attainment of Hayek's ideal—and economic recovery

The accomplishment of these four further reforms, in conjunction with the consolidation and simplification of trade union law, would mean that the state of the law was close to Professor Hayek's ideal—the revocation of the special privileges granted to the trade unions in 1906. Moreover, once it became clear that the Thatcher Government was committed to the abolition of special privileges not only for trade unions but also for *all* professional groups, including opticians and lawyers, which have developed a strongly collectivist mentality during

[77]

the 20th century, people would increasingly come to respect the law, and to become aware of the futility of Parliamentary lobbying as an economic exercise. Then the stage would be set for the economic recovery and the reduction in unemployment so generally desired.

*May/June 1984*

CHARLES G. HANSON
*Department of Economics,*
*University of Newcastle upon Tyne*

SOME PRESS COMMENT ON THE FIRST EDITION OF

# 1980s Unemployment and the Unions

'When Mr James Prior was asked at an unreported gathering in London what he thought of Professor Hayek's last Institute of Economic Affairs booklet, which blamed unemployment and other economic difficulties on union power, he is said to have replied that he did not read that sort of thing. This was in sharp contrast to Mr Frank Chapple who has bothered to give the professor a brief and—politically, if not economically— telling reply.

'This episode shows in a nutshell what is wrong with the Green Paper on Trade Union Immunities. It is written entirely from the point of view of industrial relations experts and lawyers, with no analysis at all of the economic issues.'

Samuel Brittan, *Financial Times*


'It is highly satisfactory to be able to pray in aid Professor Hayek whose pamphlet "1980s Unemployment and the Unions" argues unanswerably that "Jobs are from the beginning a product of the market". As he says of post-war Britain, "Wages are no longer determined by demand and supply but by alleged considerations of justice which means in effect not only simply custom and tradition, but increasingly sheer power". For Hayek, it has been the inordinate demands of particular power-ful unions that have been the chief source of the trouble. Had the market been truly free, had not the mercury in certain glasses been kept artificially warm and high, the general level of real wages would have been higher. The power which gave some unions monopolistic authority was a kind of property. If property is misused, other people will suffer.'

Leader, *Daily Telegraph*


'If it were possible to name one man, one Guru, one outstanding High Priest of Wisdom to whom Mrs Thatcher is always likely to listen, who would you choose? Professor Milton Friedman? Sir Keith Joseph? Or perhaps Denis Thatcher? Wrong.

'The loftiest voice from the tallest Ivory Tower of monetarism is that of an 81-year-old Austrian-born professor, Friedrich August von Hayek. Hayek is the Godfather of Free Enterprise, venerated by Conservative economists and idolised by union bashers. His simple message: Let unemployment rip until people learn the error of their ways. In 1974 he was awarded the Nobel Prize for his economics . . . The Hayek tone reached fever pitch yesterday when he published (for the IEA) a pamphlet on unemployment and the unions. In effect, this called for the abolition of the unions as we know them. An exaggeration? Well, look at this statement: "There is no hope of Great Britain maintaining her position in international trade—and for her people that means no hope of maintaining their already reduced standard of living—unless the unions are deprived of their coercive powers". '

Geoffrey Goodman, *Daily Mirror*

'There can be no economic salvation for Britain until excessive trade union privileges are revoked, says Nobel Prize winning economist Professor Friedrich Hayek in a recent paper, "1980s Unemployment and the Unions—The Distortion of Relative Prices by Monopoly in the Labour Market".

'Asked by *Accountancy* how he would limit unions' powers, which are after all conferred by law, the Austrian-born professor said that he favoured a referendum, seeking a mandate to remove all privileges granted to unions which were not held by ordinary individuals.'

*Accountancy*

'This splendid 19th-century view (presumably based on the belief that labour is a marketplace where employers go shopping for bargains) is not just irrelevant: it is also misleading and mischievous. It is misleading because the British trade-union movement, for all its undoubted faults, has virtually no legalised powers; it has merely immunities at law, the very things which the present Government has been seeking to curb through its employment legislation.'

*Engineering Today*

[80]